HERE'S
LOOKING
AT YOU,
KIDS

Also by Hugh O'Neill

Daddy Cool

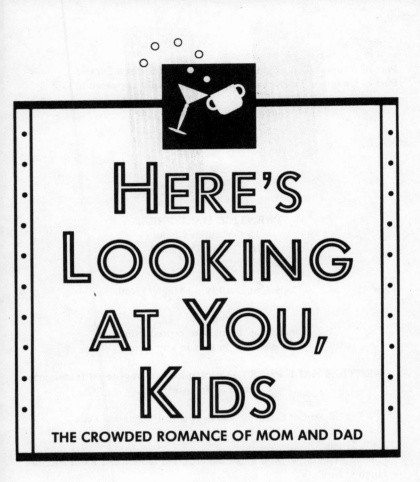

HERE'S LOOKING AT YOU, KIDS

THE CROWDED ROMANCE OF MOM AND DAD

Hugh O'Neill

Prentice
HALL
PRESS

NEW YORK LONDON TORONTO SYDNEY TOKYO SINGAPORE

Part of Chapter Ten originally appeared in *Reader's Digest*.
Part of Chapters Twelve and Eighteen originally appeared in *GQ*.

PRENTICE HALL PRESS
15 Columbus Circle
New York, NY 10023

PRENTICE HALL PRESS and colophons are registered trademarks
of Simon & Schuster, Inc.

Library of Congress Cataloging-in-Publication Data

O'Neill, Hugh.
    Here's looking at, you kids : the crowded romance of mom and dad /
Hugh O'Neill.
        p.   cm.
    ISBN 0-13-201153-0
    1. Parenting—Humor.   I. Title.
HQ755.8.053   1991
306.874'0207—dc20
                                                            90-47175
                                                            CIP

Designed by Levavi & Levavi/Carla Weise

Manufactured in the United States of America

        10   9   8   7   6   5   4   3   2   1

First Edition

To
Anne Haran O'Neill,
who wrote the music.

CONTENTS

INTRODUCTION:
This Chevy Is Bound for Glory xi

CHAPTER 1:
How to Have Every Human Emotion Before
Breakfast 1

CHAPTER 2:
Of Tiny Orations and Standing Ovations 9

CHAPTER 3:
Of Roller Coasters, Chuck Yeager, and the
Simple Courage of a Man with Kids 19

CHAPTER 4:
The Legend of Just Us 29

CHAPTER 5:
Did the Chicken Even Cross the Road? 35

CHAPTER 6:
Right Here, Over the Rainbow 41

CHAPTER 7:
Of Grand Canyons and Small Bones 49

CHAPTER 8:
Last Tango in Dayton   61

CHAPTER 9:
Of Pig Latin and Camelot   69

CHAPTER 10:
My Father Was a Mother Hen   77

CHAPTER 11:
Thanks for Everything, Big Guy   85

CHAPTER 12:
Long Ago and Far Away   95

CHAPTER 13:
Hush Little Daddy, Don't Say a Word   103

CHAPTER 14:
She Ain't Heavy, She's My Sister   115

CHAPTER 15:
My Most Unforgettable Character: Dad   121

CHAPTER 16:
Of Birthday Cake and Existential Ache   129

CHAPTER 17:
On the Facts of Life and the Tact of My Wife   139

CHAPTER 18:
How Not to Assemble a Plastic Fruit Stand
and Learn the True Meaning of Christmas   147

CHAPTER 19:
Of Money, Marketing, and My Little Pony   157

CHAPTER 20:
The Way You Wear Your Hat, The Way They
Spill Your Tea   167

CHAPTER 21:
Once Upon a "What Is Time?"   177

CHAPTER 22:
Can Daddy Come Out and Play?   185

CHAPTER 23:
Nights of Shining Ardor   203

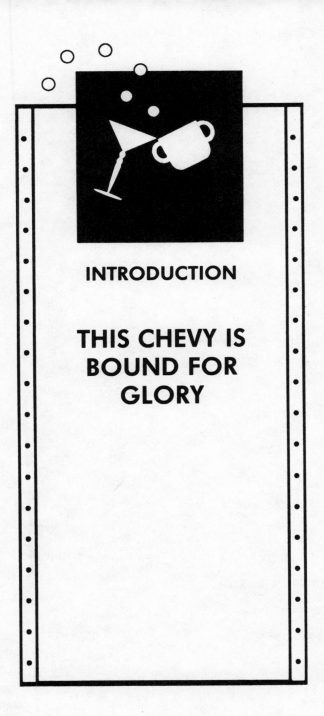

INTRODUCTION

THIS CHEVY IS BOUND FOR GLORY

I saw the truth on the New Jersey Turnpike. I was eating animal crackers at the time.

We were headed north—Philadelphia to New York—when I realized that I had just fallen in love. Not with my wife, Jody, who was asleep next to me. That passion had taken root long ago. And not with the sticky, crumb-covered kids passed out and strapped down in the backseat. But with the four of us, this team, this creature that Jody and I had conjured up, on purpose and as if by magic.

Just seven minutes before I had threatened to leave the kids at Exit 14. A minute before that, I'd been hit in the back of the head with a cookie. Just fifteen minutes earlier still, my son, Josh, had told me that he would rather live in the men's room of the Joyce Kilmer service area than get back in the car with me.

But no matter; now sleep had claimed them all with the suddenness of a fairy-tale potion, and there, inching through the hectic rain on that chemical-choked urban atrocity of wires and fumes, thumping in sleepy serenity through the anonymous near-midnight darkness of Weehawken, New Jersey, I felt suddenly less like a target for a Fig Newton than I did like Sir Lancelot, a man on a mission.

Inspired by the crowded solitude of that car and that highway, my heart and memory went rogue, careening backward through our history, then kicking into fast-forward. I imagined our twenty-two-pound daughter, Rebecca, as a Broadway producer; Josh as a high-school shortstop. I was out of control, a time traveler in a Chevrolet, enthralled by the people we had been, drunk on the adventure yet ahead.

Suddenly I saw family life clearly. Sure, it might *appear* to the outside observer that Jody and I were simply slaves to the children. It might *appear* that, far from making us the leading lady and leading man, the kids had reduced Jody to a quartermaster and me to a beast of burden. It might *appear* that we were trapped in a whorl of worry and work. But not so. After all, to this day it *appears* that the sun moves around the earth.

Now, I grant you, to see a sweaty man in a Spiderman T-shirt as a romantic hero demands more ingenuity than merely reinventing the universe. But the desperate self-aggrandizing truth I came up with at Exit 15 is that all the labor of Mom, all the lugging by Dad is nothing more than life's sleight of hand, mere illusion. The chaos of the kids in the car is camouflage for a greater and ebullient story, the legend of our gang. The backyard isn't a mess, it's Camelot. And "The Itsy-Bitsy Spider" is Beethoven's "Ode to Joy."

Since that moment of white light on the New Jersey Turnpike, I have been a domestic Don Quixote, tilting at windmills of both the figurative and the miniature-golf varieties. The family is the perennial frontier, a journey to the summit, the most daring expedition of all.

As the skyline of Manhattan swept into view across the Hudson River, I could hear the charming ache of Gershwin's love songs wafting through the fog. And when I handed a smog-numbed tollbooth operator three dollars to reenter the walled city, I said, "Thank you, my good man," in the dashing manner of Peter O'Toole as Lawrence of Arabia. I was on a crusade.

Jody awakened, warm and confused in the middle of the Lincoln Tunnel, blinking in the neon tube. She looked back at the kids, then over at me, and whispered, "What's wrong, babe?" as though the search for the Holy Grail were a problem instead of a calling.

"Nothing, doll, everything's fine," I said, with the flourish of empire. "We're almost home." Home, I thought, the same place Ulysses was headed. From that day to this, beneath the draining and delightful jazz piano of watching over the kids, I've heard the string section and the brass rising in crescendo.

The story you are about to read is the testimony of a knight of the kitchen table, the confession of a tired and grateful man. This is no country for jaded hearts, those whose swash can only be buckled by journeys across Christendom. No, this is an epic of far subtler stripe—a quilted crusade.

So if your heart isn't up to an all-day, everyday romance, consider—by the way of a consumer warning— the advice the sign on the Yellow Brick Road gave Dorothy and her pals, "I'd turn back if I were you." But if, like me, you're doomed to see the New Jersey Turnpike as the way west—the road to brand-new dreams— then welcome to a romance about laundry, about the zoo, about counting to ten in ultimatum. Welcome to a world where apple juice is nectar of the gods. Welcome to a slow dance of night-lights and snow pants. Welcome to what would be a look at family life through rose-colored glasses, if the kids hadn't sold my glasses to their friend, Phil.

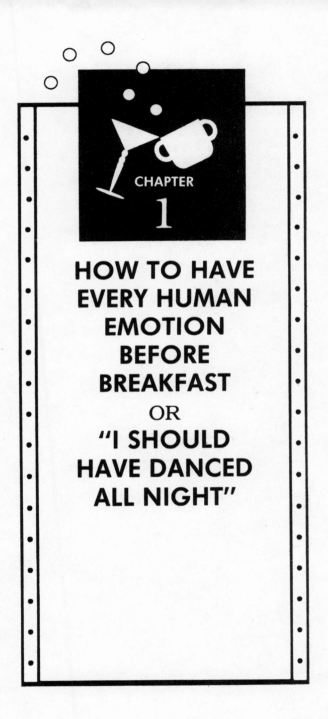

CHAPTER

1

HOW TO HAVE
EVERY HUMAN
EMOTION
BEFORE
BREAKFAST

OR

"I SHOULD
HAVE DANCED
ALL NIGHT"

The farewells were cheerful. As we shut the door on Mommy and Josh departing for the weekend, Rebecca ran over to the coffee table. "Daddy, come play wis me," she said, the *s* in lieu of *th* a verbal vestige of babyhood at two and a half.

I followed.

Looking back, I can see that was my first mistake.

She had invented what she called a "spinning game." You had to drop a little top from over your head, spinning it onto a big pottery plate and then, if I understood the game correctly, throw coins at the whirling toy. When I tried to pick up the coins from the plate, I found out that this game had other rules as well. My daughter spoke to me harshly. I put the coins back.

To say Reba liked this game doesn't get close. She laughed and jumped, no, she actually gamboled about, turning to me every nine seconds or so and saying, "Isn't this fun, Daddy?" About the game itself, the answer was "no." But it was fun seeing our girl fired by this sport of her concoction. I was dazzled by her arrogance, her pride of authorship, the ruthless baby rigor with which she insisted the game be played. I was struck more forcefully than I had ever been before by her personality. I felt uplifted, enhanced. If I knew then what I would know twenty minutes later, I would have felt endangered.

After Reba and I had scattered about three bucks in change around the living room, she stopped in midtwirl and said, "Daddy, I wanna pay wis cay." (Translation: "play with clay"). "One cay fun factory, coming right up," I said, sounding more like Shari Lewis than a guy who needed a shave.

We adjourned to her room and as I watched her making "cay cookies" I found myself impressed by her competence, the deft Zen-like care with which she arranged her equipment. I imagined her all grown up, the by-the-way-gorgeous Dr. O'Neill tying off an artery. And then, in the middle of making a harmonious stack of "cay coins," my guru said, "Dance wis me, Daddy."

Oh yes, my child, I thought. Yes, Reba, I'll dance with you all the days of my life.

And so, we danced to a medley of soft-rock radio—Carly Simon and Ronnie Millsap, I recall. As I held her—alert, robust, and sticky—in my arms, she clapped, sang along as best she could, and every three minutes or so, rested her head on my shoulder. I hoped she would remember our dance.

I fell for this in a big way. I thought of the sublime chance that had brought us here together, of my grandparents booking passage from Ireland, of Jody's people finding their way here from Russia, to this little girl. And so we danced—spinning, twirling, one of us a sniffling fool unaware of what awaited him. We danced until the older of us could dance no more.

"Daddy has to take a rest, Reb, let's read a book."

"No, Daddy, dance wis me."

"I wish I could, doll, but I'm just too tired. You wore me out."

"Daddy, dance wis me," she said again.

"Sorry, babe, I can't dance . . ."

"DADDY, DANCE WIS ME," she barked, this time a command. This can't be, I thought, the same child who eighteen seconds ago made me feel history in my heart. This rude little midget can't be the same child. She just can't be.

"DANCE WIS ME, DADDY," she said, yet again, if

anything, a decibel or two louder still. That did it. That shout had turned me into a symbol, the representative of all parents who never get credit for anything they do, but always get clobbered for the things they don't. This had gone on long enough.

"Daddy's tired, Rebecca, I can't dance," I said with a little bite of my own.

"DANCE WIS ME, DADDY!" she shrieked, apparently unaware of the ridiculous way she said *with*.

"Rebecca, that is enough dancing for today," I said, sitting down and opening a newspaper in the hope of putting an end to all this.

"DADDY, DANCE WIS ME!" she roared implacably as she came diving through the newspaper. Suddenly, the child who was ninety seconds ago licking my neck, purring into my shoulder, had become one of the Furies. I wondered for an instant if she'd gone insane, but was reassured in a flash by another goal-oriented primal scream. "I SAID, DANCE WIS ME, DADDY." I was amazed—though not scared—by the not-so-veiled threat the addition of "I said" before the command implied. Subtext: Perhaps you didn't hear what I said. This is your last warning.

By now, Rebecca was beyond the reach of a human voice. She was stretched out on the floor among the torn remnants of the *Wall Street Journal*, arms and legs rigid, possessed by tantrum. I was angry. But I don't mind admitting I was unmanned as well. I was no match for this girl. I had some ethical standards that would hobble me in an ultimate confrontation; she didn't. I fled. I locked myself in the bathroom.

I sat there on the floor, mentally listing all the reasons why I didn't deserve this. I had played the top game, helped her with clay, danced with her for half an hour. Then she must have opened her lunatic eyes long enough to notice that I'd split.

"WHERE ARE YOU, DADDY?" she howled.

"I'm in the bathroom, Reb," I answered. Why did I answer, you ask? Would Janet Leigh have answered, "I'm in the shower, Norman"? How's this for Sap of the Year honors: I answered because I didn't want her, this chubby little she-devil, to have a moment's anxiety that I'd left her alone. After all, she'd just said good-bye to Mommy and brother.

Then I heard a rush of little feet toward me, syncopated to a desperate and ferocious cry. And then, the sudden thump of a child against the bathroom door. She had hit it going full bore. There was a nanosecond of stunned silence. Flecks of paint fell from the hinges. I started to get up, to help my surely unconscious girl, but sank down under the sink again when her howl—not injured, just enraged, the shriek of the maenads—resumed.

"Let me in, Daddy," she said. Not by the hair on my chinny-chin-chin, thought I. And then it happened. I heard a faint scratching and looked down at the bottom of the door. I saw her fingers clawing their way, ferretlike, toward me. First, just her little pink-white cuticle tips, then slowly, knuckle by knuckle, a hand emerged, groping urgently across the tile, sound-tracked by her small madness. I wondered if I could get option money from Stephen King.

I reached out to push her frantic hand away and broke out laughing. I was being menaced by someone who was afraid of Captain Kangaroo. I took her hand/claw, squeezed it with what was either love or capitulation and, through what I can only call giggles, said, "It's okay, babe, I'm coming out." Unarmed, hands in the air, I might have added.

I stood up and opened the door on a diaper-clad, newsprint-streaked demon, her face mottled and tear-stained, her concave little chest heaving toward calm. I tried to look annoyed, but she saw me smile in spite of myself. She chuckled as though relieved that I'd seen exactly how funny this whole situation was.

I picked her up and we laughed nervously together at what had happened between us, or rather to each of us. She put her head on my shoulder and muttered, *sotto voce* and sheepish, "Dance wis me, Daddy."

"Pardon me, Reb?" I said, pretending not to have heard.

"Dance wis me, Daddy," she said again, aware of the game. It was, I like to believe, more of a request than a command.

Anyway, dance with her I did. Vanquished, awed, and undone. I wheeled with her around the room, telling myself that her willfulness wasn't the nightmare on earth it seemed. It was actually a good sign, so went my desperate musing, and would eventually power a life of her own invention. We danced until the steady rales of sleep on my neck told me that the victor had given herself over to a well-earned rest.

Mythologist Joseph Campbell has written that people are after not the meaning of life but just some evidence that they are alive. And thinking back on how I had been poleaxed by my daughter, I consoled myself with the thought that I had raced through the wardrobe of emotions—affection, gratitude, rage, fear, hope, delight, and hilarity—within the time it takes to boil an egg. I was alive, all right.

To parents, this kind of roller coaster is just the stuff of Tuesday afternoon. Mom and Dad are the Dionysian daredevils of Maple Road, able to move from euphoria to dread at warp speed. The sudden topography of parenthood—the unexpected ups, the ambush of the downs—marks Mom and Dad clearly. These people have been through something, probably within the last few minutes.

Having kids is a pendulum of exuberance and pixilation, a ticktock of elation and droop. It leaves you breathless and confused. Why, it's almost like being in love.

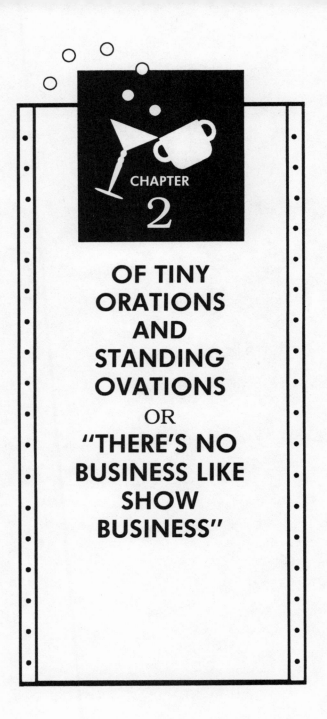

CHAPTER

2

**OF TINY
ORATIONS
AND
STANDING
OVATIONS**

OR

**"THERE'S NO
BUSINESS LIKE
SHOW
BUSINESS"**

Ever since Josh turned five I've considered myself an honorary member of Actors Equity, the troupe roomy enough to enfold both Jessica Tandy and Sean Penn. Four times a week I'm dragooned—or should I say, invited—by Josh, our own Joe Papp, Jr., to escape the humdrum world of work and wage and be part of a rabbit's great adventure or the peopling of Venus.

Sometimes I carry a spear and sometimes I carry the show. I've been called on to create a range of roles that would have challenged the great Sir Laurence himself. I've done some nice work as a frog princess, a less than Oscar-quality stint as a magic stone, and a downright brave—and, I might add, underappreciated—turn as the island of Jamaica. Along the way I've learned a few parental thespian lessons, which I offer here without prescription, but with modest faith that prepared is better than bushwhacked.

• Whatever your role, the kids will insist that you perform it in the most physically demanding way possible. Once I tried to do the West Wind while sitting down—waving my arms in a modified hula and blowing eerily, icily across the room. Josh was underwhelmed. "No, Daddy, like this," he said, as he squatted down, stretched his arms straight out in front of him, moved his head from side to side, and hoo-hooed as he waddled, ducklike, forward, a little feathered minstrel. Nobody over eleven years old can do this. All I got for my trouble was a muscle spasm; Mommy (the understudy) got her big break.

• The kids will always insist that you recite your lines word for word. If you say "the land of evil giants" when you were told to say "the land of bad giants," they'll stop the play to set you straight. Kids are not much for vamping. They'll be all over you about the most minor rewrite.

• Daddy always plays the fall guy. Eight out of ten characters fathers play will end badly—tied up, squished, run through by Ivanhoe, taunted by a pig-tailed mob. Not to worry. First of all, I'm sure that vanquishing Dad has some therapeutic upside for their little oedipal hearts. And second, nobody ever got famous playing nice. There's no percentage in playing Goody Two-Shoes; Iago is the career-maker.

Though it's tough to imagine anything worse than having to render a cranky caterpillar, some parents would argue that having a part—however torturous—is better than being trapped in the audience for a puerile production. Consider this story of two men and two women watching four children tread the boards.

It started with a two o'clock invitation from my eight-year-old niece, Austin, clearly the executive producer. "We're having a show, an Easter Show, at five o'clock in the playroom. All mothers and fathers are welcome to attend." It was followed by parental huzzahs of expectation.

Cut to 5 P.M., a darkened basement room, folding chairs arranged in mom-and-dad rows, and handmade crayoned programs that read:

The O'Neill Theatre Presents
The Adventures of Pippi Longstocking

The lights come up on a minimalist set, revealing the producer's six-year-old sister as announcer. "Ladies and gentlemen, we are proud to present *The Adventures of Pippi Longstocking, An Easter Show.*"

With that, Austin, in the role of Pippi, comes back-flipping onto the stage, an eye-catching, athletic entrance, more Mary Lou Retton than Meryl Streep.

"Hello," she shouts, "I'm Pippi Longstocking and this is the story of my adventures. The first thing Pippi does," she continues *en haut voix*, "is wash the car."

Wash the car?

Pippi Longstocking?

Out rush her three colleagues and they do a mad mime version of scrubbing down a Grand Am. We know they're washing the car because Pippi just told us. We all smile in affectionate amusement, imagining the kids talking over how to start the show and actually coming up with the Turtle Wax opening bit.

After either two minutes or two years of hosing and buffing, Pippi does an Olympic-quality handspring stage left and our Rebecca, cast as someone named "Laura, the substitute," comes downstage and says, "The second thing Pippi does is get her braces fixed."

I feel the entire audience go numb. My sister-in-law clutches my arm and whispers, "Oh, my God." I'll never forget her voice. It was a German expressionist painting—a bleak cry in the dark. We all knew at once that Pippi's adventures were going to be not a chain of events linked in a great tale, not a story, a narrative—but a series of stand-alone experiences that marked the mundane progress of a little girl through a homework-and-car-maintenance day.

Time slowed down.

When we learned that Pippi was going to get a perm, I patted my sister-in-law's white-knuckled hand reassuringly, though my despair was as deep as hers. As we watched Laura, the substitute, race around Pippi,

madly mixing up her hair with her fingers, time
stopped.

Then Pippi brushed her teeth. Then she walked her
dog. (The dog was played by Laura, the substitute. The
other two were well-wishers in the park. "Good morning, Pippi, have a nice day," they squeaked in unison.)
When Pippi finished her lunch, my brother, Kevin, in a
move of ingenious desperation, jumped up and
shouted, "Hooray, bravo, what a wonderful play!" The
kids looked at him as though he were simple and Pippi
shouted, "No, Daddy, the show's not over." Daddy sat
down and thought, I'm sure, of Dante's inferno.

Pippi called her swimming coach.

Pippi jumped rope.

Pippi gave the dog a bath.

The seasons changed.

When Pippi started on her math homework, Jody
jumped up suddenly and said, "Oops, there's the
phone, I'll get it." None of us had heard a ring, but my
sister-in-law said, "I better help you with that, Jode,"
and drifted out of the room in Jody's wake.

Only Kevin and I remained. Fitting, I thought. We'd
been a pair from the start. And there in that airless
basement, I thought of the baseball days of our youth,
the supple bones and big dreams of being American
boys together. I looked over at my all-grown-up brother,
who had always, it seemed, been by my side. I gagged
on the irony that we would die here together in the
basement with our wives upstairs pretending to talk on
the phone.

Pippi did a back-flip.

Pippi ate a Popsicle.

Pippi gave that damn dog some kibble.

The Grand Canyon got a tad deeper.

Kevin suddenly stood up again, swept some dried
flowers out of a vase in the bookcase, handed them

with a quick flourish to Laura, the substitute, and shouted, "Author, author, bravo!" Pippi somersaulted downstage in protest again, but the other three, I suspect tired of being fifth business to Pippi's star turn, suddenly lined up and took a bow. Kevin and I hooted and whooped and whistled. The kids thought we loved the show. In fact, we loved each other.

Just as the show ended I searched my mental file for the upside of what had just happened. Beyond my niece's acrobatic gifts, I could, at first, find no silver lining. I could think of no way that any of us—adult or child—had been enhanced, redeemed by this suffering.

But later that night nature's generosity showed itself. Pippi's mother walked past me in the kitchen and gave me a spur-of-the-moment half hug. It was a gesture born of two bonds: one trivial—we loved my brother with everything we had—and one profound— we had peeked together, side by side, into the Pippi Longstocking abyss.

TO BE OR NOT TO BE THE BIG BAD WOLF

A week after the Pippi Longstocking debacle, my optimistic glands had healed and I found myself sitting in yet another audience. This time I was in a school gym, amid the fragrance of banana-scented programs, which are the only thing in the world that hasn't changed since JFK and Jackie were king and queen.

The kids were up there on stage, doing a musical called *Madame Curie: A Woman for All Time.* It appeared to have a personal hygiene subplot. There was a tooth-decay patter song that two eight-year-olds did with Rooney-Garland style.

Suddenly, watching a portly lad swagger through a clearly heavyset and jovial role, I realized the importance of paying attention to the roles in which your kids are cast. It's not important whether he's the leading man or a bit player, but it is important to be sure he's not typecast before he even has a chance to turn into a type.

Consider: Josh's first role was as the merchant who sold The Three Little Pigs their building supplies. Not too demanding, but a pivotal role nonetheless. Those porkers don't get their straw and bricks, and we're looking at a not-much story. But when I asked Josh who was going to be the Big Bad Wolf I really knew the answer. "Brendan," he said, as though I shouldn't have had to ask. You see, Brendan was Miss Crabtree's problem boy. Clearly, the minute she thought Big Bad Wolf, Brendan came to mind. Now, she meant no harm. She loves Brendan in her way, though he is a handful. But the point is that by age five Brendan's future was assured. He'll be the Big Bad Wolf his whole life. He may even use it as an alias.

Early on, be sure that your child—whether thug or sprite—is cast *against* type. If your son is a pip-squeak, ask Miss Crabtree to try him as something other than a Christmas elf. If your daughter is a linebacker, insist on pixie and not the zaftig Mrs. Claus. Even if we could know anything about the future, it's just too early to start telling them what kind of people they are. Remember, this is Act One.

In all the world there's nothing like watching your child in a play. Every three minutes you'll find yourself about to jump out of your seat and shout a cue, "But Pierre, *mon cher,* don't you see, it emits particles."

There she is up on stage, every emotion in the human repertoire—embarrassment, pride, terror, self-assertion—surging at once through her little body. Declaiming her lines with purpose, shuffling her feet with fear, she's somehow both sheepish and bold. A child in a play is a metaphor for it all—our longing for attention, our fear of ridicule, our sweetness, our tenacity, our dread that we'll forget our lines.

Watching the kid hit her marks is an unendurable pleasure.

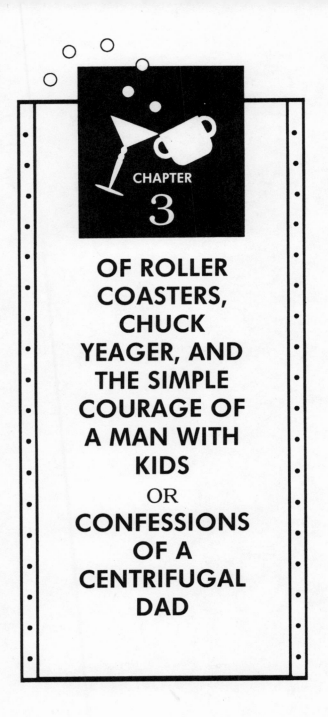

OF ROLLER COASTERS, CHUCK YEAGER, AND THE SIMPLE COURAGE OF A MAN WITH KIDS

OR

CONFESSIONS OF A CENTRIFUGAL DAD

Once you become a father you sign away your claim on the uncharted parts of the world. You agree not to split in search of the source of the Nile, to light out for the territory, or to have any of the bold self-reliant adventures that have merely owned your subconscious since you first slapped on a coonskin cap back when we all liked Ike. No, once you're a father you agree to stop dreaming Lewis and Clark dreams; you agree to stay home and work on the lawn.

But for men, the siren's whisper, the call of the wild isn't easily subdued. You can't just *agree* not to have an adrenal gland. And in fact, Mother Nature wants Dad to keep his edge. So she presents him with occasional and unlikely forums to showcase the physical audacity of the take-it-to-the-limit boys. Springing now and then out of the hither and yon of being with children, these moments are pop quizzes on manhood, nature's way of making sure that Dad can still be trusted with the kids.

The story of our day at the amusement park is the story of such a test. Though it may sound at first like the merely buoyant reminiscence of a family on a lark, it ends with a dark night of body and soul, a physical trial that would have had G. Gordon Liddy begging for mercy. This is the story of a day that starts with the children singing "Heigh-ho, heigh-ho" and ends with Dad seeing Goyaesque visions.

But before turning to the daddy art of testing limits—in the parlance of Chuck Yeager, "stretching the envelope"—bear with me through a cheerful, if self-serving, lament, an editorial/confession about carnival corruption and fatherly pride.

GAMES OF SKILL OR A MARK FOR A SHILL?

The so-called games of skill at amusement parks are tough on fathers. They are often the first chance your kids get to watch you fail extravagantly and in plain sight. They are also an unreported national scandal. For the fact is that your chances of winning a prize from the top shelf are about the same as Walter Mondale's of getting another shot at being chief executive.

Now, my wife will tell you these are the maunderings of a bad sport, and she'll add—not because anybody needs to know, but because she believes humility is good for the soul, or rather for my soul—that I've never won the kids anything but a plastic whistle. This is both vicious and untrue. She conveniently forgets the finger puppet I bagged, thank you very much, at the hospital fair Golf Ball Roll.

But she doesn't understand. Nor does any woman understand. Because it's never Mom up there trying to toss a Ping-Pong ball into an odd-numbered thimble. No, it's never Mom who's asked to slide a sticky puck across a rubber mat. No, Mom is the one standing just to your left, apparently unaware that fully half of those stuffed dolls are actually cemented to the shelves on which they appear to perch so precariously and that another 25 percent of them are on springed hinges that pop them back up even after you've nailed them dead center with your heater.

Oh sure, the guy running the booth can pick up three balls and, while offering a crocodile consolation to Dad, casually knock off three dolls. But that's because he controls the switch that disconnects the hinges.

I'm stumped. Somehow my wife, who has raised suspicion of politicians and investment bankers to an art, is willing to believe that the guy with the tattoo named Randy is Thurgood Marshall. "Hugh, have you noticed all those kids carrying those big bears?" Jody once asked me, as though she didn't know those tykes were shills, juvenile hoodlums in the pay of Fagin, the carny owner. She even once pointed out a parish priest carrying a giant panda, as though she'd never heard of the old Father Flanagan come-hither.

But no matter. My wife's gullibility is her problem. Herewith—before getting to the story of how I was tested at high noon—a few hard-earned lessons about the old three-for-a-dollar, win-your-boy-a-bear softball throw.

DADDY CLUES FOR THE COMPETITIVE EDGE

1. Those target dolls are narrower than the five or six inches they appear to be. In fact most of the width is fuzz, through which the ball will just whiz, doing no damage. This optical illusion—or should I say this fraud that the department of consumer protection should look into—suckers some fathers into aiming on a broad horizontal plane, hoping to get lucky as to longitude. Won't work. Your only slim hope is to go dead center on a particular doll with each throw.

2. Don't sacrifice velocity for accuracy. The dolls that aren't on hinges are filled with mercury, which is among the heaviest of the naturally occurring metals. I've seen dozens of trusting fathers take a nice

easy Tommy John windup, only to have their hurls
clonk off a battlement that looks for all the world like
a straw-and-sawdust totem from the Caribbean.
3. Don't even consider playing a carnival game until you've just watched for a few hours.' Make
mental—hell, even written—notes of which dolls
you've actually seen knocked over. Observe the flight
path of the eccentric balls. You might even talk to
another father or two about whether they sail or dive,
slide right or hook left. Get as much information as
you can. Gamesmanship is about small edges. Remember, if you fail with Frank, Jr., by your side, he'll
endure a double-barreled disappointment about
something he doesn't have—the life-size bear—and
something he does—a father who couldn't throw his
express past Princess Di.

There is another kind of carnival game that is—in its
way—more pernicious than the merely fixed. I'm talking, of course, about the amusement park game that
isn't crooked, but just impossibly difficult. The most
dramatic example is called "Hammer the Frog onto the
Spinning Lily Pad." I came across it for the first time in
south Jersey, but it's got cousins ("Heave the Skunk
into the Whirling Burrow") all over the country.
The daddy assignment is merely this: Using a rubber
hammer, whack one end of a tabletop seesaw in such a
way that the rubber frog sitting on the other end arcs
through the air and onto a lily pad that is:

1. Half the size of the frog, and
2. Moving at light speed around a little metal tabletop frog pond.

Part of the problem is mental. When we see a green
rubber frog, our minds think fun and games. But this
isn't about a good time, this is about trajectory and

throw-weight. In fact, the last father to win his daughter a life-size lamb gave up a teacher's pension, and went to work for DOD on a project he still can't talk about.

But enough about failure. On to the point, the story of a day at the amusement park and a stoic, if staggering, success.

I should have been suspicious from the get-go. The day started out with just too much promise. No mere Saturday could possibly sustain the good cheer that was our house as we prepared for the outing to Fantasyland. Josh and Rebecca bounced around, pulling on overalls with verve, brushing their teeth without coaxing. Jody put her hair back in pink dinosaur barrettes—Sandra Dee as American Mom. Even the weather was perfect—summer giving way to fall, a duet of bright sun and cool breeze. As we clambered into the car that morning I felt strong, ready for life, at the peak of my powers—in my mid-thirties, both a little youthful and a little wise. It was the pride that wenteth before the fall.

We arrived at Shangri-La and the kids were mute with excitement. Josh couldn't make any noise at all; he could only squirm. Rebecca settled for jumps and squeaks.

We paid what I remember as seven thousand dollars for four all-day, every-ride-in-the-place-as-often-as-you-like bracelets, and stood for a moment, getting our bearings, at the entrance crossroads. I thought of the phrase Francis Parkman used to describe his first steps onto the Oregon Trail, "jumping off," heading into the delicious and dangerous unknown.

We rode on a swaying dragon. I looked the fool on some Lilliputian motorboats. The kids bounced around from ride to ride, reluctant to settle on any one lest they have to wait to try another. I think I first felt dizzy after the caterpillar ride. We plunged on. After a bouncing session on a great inflatable thing for bouncing, we headed for the Tilt-A-Whirl.

The Tilt-A-Whirl, all multihued and cheerful, was the Rubicon. I stumbled as I stepped out of the Humpty-Dumpty seat and, though I caught myself before falling flat, it was a bad omen. After the Tilt-A-Whirl, there was no going back. Destiny lay ahead.

The kids were on fire now, gaining courage with each ride, talking with bravado about the roller coaster that had terrified them just ten minutes before. The bio-chemical messages from my brain said, "Take a break, boyo." The kids said, "The Scrambler looks great, Dad, let's go."

As we lined up for the Scrambler, Jody said, "Hugh, you look a little pale. Maybe you should skip this ride?" I chuckled with as much condescension as I could muster without throwing up and sneered, "Yeah, and Yeager took a skip on the acceleration trials."

Jody watched from the sidelines as onto the Scrambler we went—my forty-eight-pound boy on one side, my thirty-one-pound girl on the other, a sheltering paternal arm around each. Slowly, the beast began to move. We whirled in a tight circle around a nearby pole and in a great planetary arc around the main axis of the Scrambler.

Within seven seconds I knew I was in the wrong spot. Even in the first easygoing turn centrifugal force had its relentless way with me, and my weight smushed softly against Rebecca. I couldn't switch places with her—the gaily painted safety bar held us like a vise.

I remember saying a prayer. I may have said something to God about missionary work if we all walked away. I cursed myself for a fool. I kissed my kids on their heads in farewell. And then I waited, waited as the speed picked up, throwing me with increasing force against my little girl. She looked up at me and laughed. She thought Daddy was just being silly. The little dopey angel had made a big mistake—she'd trusted the old man.

Two more turns and she said, "Move over, Daddy, you're squishing me." Reaching around Josh's head I grabbed the other side of the car desperately. But my arms couldn't resist the force that flung me outward. I remembered—in the way one recalls fragments in moments of in extremis—doing a duck puzzle with Rebecca the week before and how the afternoon sun had illuminated her face and the duck's feet. I slid once again against the babe. "Daddy, stop it, you're squishing me," she said again. I thought of the Donner party. Finally, Rebecca, God bless her rage, got mad. "Daddy!" she shouted, this time suddenly standing up in annoyance. I slid quickly underneath her and wrapped my arms around her. I pushed myself against the outside of the car. We were going to make it.

When the Scrambler finally stopped, the kids hopped out, giddily unaware of what had just happened. They bounded toward Mommy as I staggered over to the guy running the ride, a citizen's arrest on my mind. I asked him how he could in conscience operate a ride that killed dozens of kids and parents weekly. He said, "Take a hike, cap'n." I doubled over and put my hands on my knees. I tried to pretend I was looking for a contact lens. A nice woman in shorts and a straw hat started crawling around at my feet. Jody led me away.

"Are you all right, Hugh?" she said, patting me on the back.

"Oh, sure, I'm fine," I barked, shrugging her spectator's arm off my back. "I just nearly crushed our little girl."

"It's OK, Hugh, everything's OK," she said, still wearing those dumb pink dinosaur barrettes. Who did she

think she was—Sandra Dee? "Rebecca's fine. She
wants to ride the Scrambler again."

I fell to my knees and looked around at the oblivious,
happy, cotton-candy-carrying crowd. I remember
thinking that Hitchcock was right about the sinister
thump beneath the good-natured calliope of every day.

Jody drove home. I was asleep within ten minutes,
an out-of-balance thirty-five-year-old who had spun too
fast, changed direction too quickly, not just stretched
but ripped the envelope. I passed out in comatose grav-
itational tribute to Isaac Newton. I had dream visions
of looking over the edge, of Neil Armstrong and Edmund Hilary, steely-eyed, impassioned, hardy men who
had put themselves to the test, men who in daring
death had tasted life to its fullest.

When I awoke, cool now but still clammy, a ticket
stub from the dodge 'em cars was squeezed in my hand.
I looked in the mirror, forgave myself the wisp of cotton
candy worn as a blue mustache, and allowed myself a
puny pride that in my moment of trial I had not been
found wanting. Woozy? Yes. Grouchy? Absolutely. On
the verge of throwing up? To be sure. But wanting?
No, not this cowboy.

CHAPTER

4

THE LEGEND
OF JUST US

Romantic parents believe in legends, tales that fuel our faith, inspire our dedication. The family, properly imagined, is nothing less than a customized Arthurian code.

Among the most important parental skills is the art of nourishing the family myth. Any mom or dad who aspires to extravagance had better know something about the art of turning family history into *The Sword in the Stone*. To that end, a recipe for cooking up a family fable.

THE SOURCE LEGEND: "MY HEART WENT BOOM WHEN I CROSSED THAT ROOM"

Chief among the legends that organize a culture—whether ancient Aztec or yours—is what anthropologists call the source legend. In connection with a family this is also known as "The Story of How Mom and Dad Met." In any properly romantic family this should be a Kismet tale, some charming blend of serendipity and inevitability, a head-over-heels, love-at-first-sight story that leads in your kids.

Now in generations gone by this kind of amorous thunderbolt was not uncommon. The legend of my mother and father actually featured a high-school dance, World War II, and two teenagers played by Jimmy Stewart and June Allyson. But nowadays, romantic histories are often more circuitous, how shall I say, less chivalric. But even if the actual meeting wasn't of *Casablanca* quality, we nonetheless owe the children an enriching origin tale.

Here are the ingredients of an ennobling source legend:

- The first meeting should be linked to an epochal historical event—the moon landing, the day Nixon resigned, the bicentennial celebration, the day Hank Aaron caught his Babe. The debut of Mom and Dad *à deux* requires a drum roll.
- It must involve some preternatural coincidence. Mom and Dad meet as though magically. Destiny should bring them together, not Aunt Molly.
- A hat. Whether it's a leather gaucho, an Atlanta Braves baseball cap, or a derby, Dad's first memory of Mom's face is haloed by a hat. God is in the details.
- From the moment Dad sees Mom, life is changed forever. He says he likes the name Matthew for a boy, Ellen for a girl. She's charmed by his ardor, but has a late date and really has to go.

Now it's not advisable to make a big deal out of the source legend. Indeed, it should be husbanded, mentioned only in passing from time to time, if the kids insist. It should have an element of mystery. But the implicit message has to be that Mom and Dad were dynamite from Day One, that they were born in a fire that continues to heat the house.

I know, I hear the argument. Why give the kids the cockeyed thought that only the white light of sudden irresistible love will do?

Because they're entitled.

SOURCE LEGEND QUIZ

Which of the following scenarios is worthy of the romantic mom and dad?

1. You're in Grand Central Station when the news comes over the loudspeaker that the Japanese have surrendered. The boys are coming home. You turn and embrace the stranger walking past. You nearly knock her funny little Bette Davis hat off her head. Life is changed forever.

2. You and Mom meet through a singles club called "Find-a-Mate" and date for two years mostly just because nobody better comes along. But then you eventually decide to get married under the influence of Mom's biological clock.

3. You're walking glumly along the road with your sax, having just been fired from your job as a sideman at the Blue Parrot. Suddenly a Ford roadster comes swooping around a curve and you leap out of its way, tumbling down an embankment. Ten seconds later you look up and see—outlined against the setting sun at the crest of the hill—a woman in a hat you only later learn is called a cloche. The earth stops spinning.

4. You're a college freshman trying to invent a major in cool. But then one nothing-special Tuesday at a nothing-special lunch in a student cafeteria that can only be described as less than legendary, you hear a woman-girl laugh, look over to the next table and see—wearing a lime-green embroidered minidress and holding forth with spirit—a fellow student who has no idea that the father of her someday children, John and Rebecca, will shortly be following her to the dessert table.

Answer 2 is alas symptomatic of modern times. Answers 1 and 3 will do fine for family genesis. But answer 4—though it has neither the requisite memorable date, the charming coincidence, nor the hat—is the most romantic moment I can remember.

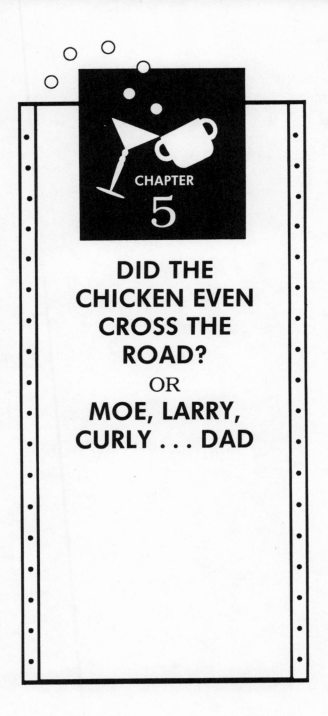

CHAPTER 5

DID THE CHICKEN EVEN CROSS THE ROAD?

OR

MOE, LARRY, CURLY . . . DAD

Wit is the spice of romance. Its expressions are various. Some couples rely on a snappy Tracy-and-Hepburn patter, others speak a more private language of love, trading bon mots less accessible to the outsider looking in. At bottom, all pairs rely on some form of secret comic sharing, a resonance that bubbles up through the routine and keeps them tuned to each other's frequency.

But as soon as Rhett and Scarlett have kids, a humorous time bomb starts ticking away. A crisis is coming, a crisis that can eventually imperil a parent's—usually Dad's—ability to hold up his end of the spousal repartee on which great romances are built.

Half a dozen years into parenthood Dad has to make a cruel choice between loyalty to his wife and the mature sense of humor that has linked him to her and comic loyalty to his kids, otherwise known as Moe, Larry, and Curly.

Long about age six or seven, eight out of ten kids (nine out of ten boys) turn into tiny shtickmeisters. They develop a huge delight in bad gags, riddles of the "Why did the chicken cross the road?" variety. More to the point, for some reason they always invite Dad to join them on the zany lane to laughs. Mom is most often seen as too grown up for big yucks. But the kids seem to somehow know that Dad once actually thought *Mad* magazine was funny, that when Dad was a lad he was what the Sisters of Mercy used to call a "card."

It all starts out innocently enough. You laugh at a five-hundred-pound-gorilla joke because you know the kids want you to. But it escalates quickly, and before you know it you're caught in a ruthless downward spiral. To wit:

- You ask a senior vice-president at work if he knows how to make an elephant float. (Answer: One glass of seltzer, two scoops of ice cream, and a smallish elephant.)
- After rinsing your hair in the shower you take two minutes to work on a few armpit sound effects.
- You buy your wife an anniversary present at a place called Mister Rollo's Novelty Shoppe.
- It's made of rubber.
- You end a dispute with a lawyer saying, "I know you are, but what am I?"
- You think you made your point.

In short, in a mere matter of weeks you can devolve from Oscar Wilde to Oscar the Grouch. My own demise bottomed out with a Bullwinkle joke occasioned by nothing more than a maître d' saying "chocolate mousse." Even the busboy was ten years too old to be amused.

My two most vivid marital memories circumscribe my comic undoing.

Number one happened ten years ago: I'm dancing with my wife, forty minutes after "I do," and she whispers that Cary Grant could take lessons from me. Number two happened one Thursday in March 1989: Jody described me to her mother as "not unlike Pee Wee Herman." In thrall to juvenile jocosity, I had gone from leading man to pseudoman.

The descent to daffy is dreary enough but the denouement is more dreadful still. No sooner have you dismantled the mordant or buoyant or rapierlike wit that had enriched your marriage than the children get serious on you. Overnight, they lose interest in X-ray specs and dribble glasses. You tell them your latest Super Pickle joke and they act like they're William F. Buckley, Jr., and this is "Firing Line." And there you are, a thirty-five-year-old given to the phrase, "I'm rubber, you're glue." There you are—sophomoric, seduced, and abandoned.

Still, even with the humiliating luxury of hindsight, I don't see how fathers can take another path. You can't just decline the kids' invitation to get goofy. If you appear unmoved by the phony wax teeth young Fred wears down to breakfast, the boy will feel cheated at least all day long, perhaps for the rest of his natural life. Every hunch I have tells me that, at least for a while, the kids need some comic companionship from the old man.

Damage control is the best you can hope for. If you're prepared for the sudden switch back to sober, you can get back on Mom's comic wavelength before she actually starts denying that on a February night with hope in the air and strawberries in the champagne, she mentioned you in the same breath with Cary Grant.

Here's a three-step plan for recovery. No guarantees, but it helped me.

CORNBALL ANONYMOUS: THE ROAD BACK

• Don't speak for days at a time. Juvenile jokes rely on a momentum of what Woody Allen called "jejunosity." Like the first drink, the first "Gotcha last" of the day can cascade into craziness. Reasserting the strong silent type you planned to be will drive away the spirit of guffaw.

• Obsess about Ralph Nader. You might even call

him if you get a sec. There's nothing funny about a Pinto bursting into flame.

● First thing each morning, rub a wire brush across the top of your fist, then suck the wound. Type O doesn't taste funny.

As with everything in family life, there is a silver lining to the nutty nightmare. Once the kids come through their low-road courtship with humor, and Dad is well again, the family as a whole can start building a comic history. Without a thought, the bunch of you turn the silly daily moments into family myth. What begins as a hodgepodge collection of one-liners—catchphrases from a tollbooth in Ohio or a Tuesday in the kitchen— grows with time into a unique treasury of reference, a sweet language of allusion that amuses no one but the guys on your team.

The family from which I come, the team on which I'm "Hughie," is gifted with a liturgy of laughter that is not the slightest bit funny to anybody who wasn't at the Little League All-Star Game in 1963. Indeed, even now—no, especially now—with everybody all grown up and thriving, gathered around the same dining-room table that hosted the yawp of youth, even now, the old just-us in-jokes endorse our loyalty and summon our unreasonable affection.

And to the team on which I'm "Dad," a phrase that is nonsense to all but four people in the world ("Obel dis") is a surefire through-the-decades laugh line, just one of the pieces that mark us as the only Hugh O'Neill—Jody Friedman coproduction in history.

RIGHT HERE, OVER THE RAINBOW

Most of the time the work can drown out the sound of the charge. It's easy for Mom and Dad to feel more like Milne's downtrodden Eeyore than like crusaders of yore. Nine times out of ten, romantic hero seems like a typo; romantic zero is closer to the truth.

But, mothers and fathers of America, I commend you to a conceited and prideful perspective. Trust me. Your ventures add up to the greatest story never told. Backyard achievements go unacknowledged only because we lack a language of domestic courage. We're stuck lavishing praise on the conqueror, instead of the real hero, the guy who can get his kids to eat beets.

Every day, moms and dads stand up to body blows that would drop Rocky Balboa. Consider the unrecorded but Olympian physical achievements that are but the routine stuff of family life.

- A father who once carried his daughter (estimated weight, forty-three pounds) on his shoulders from just outside Lincoln, Nebraska to what must have been Honesdale, Pennsylvania. Scientists believe this is the aerobic equivalent of running eight marathons in sequence, then swimming the English Channel.
- A mother who, on Tuesday, November 7, 1989, cooked seven different dinners for her kids in search of something, anything, they'd eat. By 8 P.M., she had washed 107 plates.
- A mother who tucked her son in 228 times in the thirty sleep days from mid-May to mid-June 1990.

- A father who read the worst children's book ever written out loud thirty-seven times one fall weekend last year. And why? Because his kids—God save them—love this dopey, narrow-minded, poorly rhymed, drearily illustrated, claustrophobia-inducing smear on the escutcheon of American publishing.

The world has changed. The geographical frontier is gone. And the adventurous thirsts of the future will be slaked not by exotic lands, not by distant horizons, but by acuity of vision, by seeing the kids more clearly. Home is the new beginning—the place where a fella might just build himself a life.

Those dirty dishes aren't—I swear—just another after-dinner chore. They're part of a years-long labor that enhances Mom and Dad as surely as Hercules's tasks ennobled him. Of course, you've got to look at the sink from a particular angle. But facts are facts. Laundry is, in fact, no less heroic than blazing an overland trail.

It's no surprise that we don't see ourselves as heroes—leading man and leading lady. Parents are imprisoned by the two ancestral enemies of romance: (1) stuff and (2) routine. Ask yourself. Could Rhett have escorted Scarlett upstairs with a barrel of Lincoln Logs under his arm? Would the balcony scene from *Romeo and Juliet* have endured through the ages if it had included a badminton set? Would Leander have had time to drown for love of Hero if it had been his turn in the soccer-practice car pool? The answers are no, no, and no.

The lover of myth is deliciously unencumbered. But Mom and Dad, on the contrary, are poster kids for encumbrance. If we suddenly throw our arms around any-thing, there will be Gummy Bears all over the room.

I'm always carrying something. And it's rarely a bou-quet. One afternoon last summer, when I noticed that people were giving me a wide berth on the sidewalk, I looked down to discover that I was holding an eighteen-inch-tall vulcanized plastic doll by her left foot. The kids were at home. The doll was naked. And though there was a very good explanation, the pedestrians were, understandably, ill at ease.

If the playpens and car seats weren't enough to sup-press our romance glands, the over-and-over-again re-lentlessness of the kids surely would be. The routine is not romantic. Nature may abhor a vacuum, but Mom and Dad can't live without one.

But even weighted down as we are by equipment and repetition, we need not give up our breathless schemes. There are no excuses. "The mind," wrote Milton, "is its own place." And so, in the spirit of mind over stuff and obligation, I offer mental maintenance meditations that can—in family life's most cluttered venues and routine *mise-en-scènes*—help you understand that your life is not hopelessly disenchanted by Tinkertoys and one-more-time, that you could, if necessary, give Scarlett a hand getting up to her room.

The Backseat of the Chevy

A sense of family history will come in handy. You see, the foot-deep rubble obscuring the floor mats isn't the detritus of two thoughtless tots, it's an archive of your travels. The petrified Granola Bars are the trip to see brand-new nephew Brian, the desiccated boxes of Ha-waiian Punch are that weekend at the shore. The cray-ons reek of Christmas, the shredded book that un-pleasantness at Valley Forge.

Shopping: On Bringing Home the Bacon
. . . and the Taco Chips

To the untutored eye it just looks like the frozen food aisle—chopped broccoli, orange juice, Popsicles, packaged and presented for the picking by any wimp with legal tender. Not so. It's the veld, a grassy African plain, home to springbok and zebras. And you're not fifteen pounds heavier than Dr. Rappaport says you ought to be, you're a lean, well-muscled, and nearly naked warrior charged with bringing home dinner for the little members of the tribe.

True enough, there is no physical challenge beyond pushing a heavy shopping cart. But you've already met the Darwinian test. You went out there in the world and, by doing what you do, somehow got your mitts on enough dough to bring home some oats and raisins. Now, I grant you, lots of people make a living—that's no great coup. But not everybody has a pair of totally unproductive little tribesmen at home. Not everybody is charged with getting the next generation enough iron and vitamins to give them the strength to invent the things that will have to be invented if the tribe is to survive.

So, as you're prowling through the gaudy Great American Supermarket, get primitive. Imagine that your golf shirt is a loincloth, that you're carrying a club. As you effortlessly harvest a nice head of lettuce, imagine instead that you've used your ingenuity to find the sweet reeds that the kids back in the village love.

Remember: Take pride in bringing home the bacon and the bagels. Try to picture the children's bones and muscles growing, firming up with each bite they take courtesy of you. Pay no attention to that special on canned tuna. This isn't the Winn Dixie; it's a hunting-gathering adventure.

Laundry: Of Colorfast and Steadfast

We live in a world of spin and rinse. The shimmy of the washing machine is the bass line of the family song. I grant you, yet another pile of laundry is not the stuff dreams are made of. But maybe that's not just the Bosco-stained mountain of corduroy and denim it appears to be. Maybe it's a stack of military uniforms, the raiments of yesterday's battle. And maybe you're no slave to detergent and bleach, no modest beater of garments on rocks. Maybe you're the quartermaster, charged with presenting the troops, festooning them to take the field. And maybe that's not a T-shirt promoting the Indiana Pacers but an officer's tunic. And that no careless clot of ketchup but a red badge of courage.

And maybe folding those teensy little brontosaurus slacks isn't just a tedious, mind-numbing necessity, but a test of dexterity and precision. And maybe, just maybe, it will prepare you for a midlife career switch. After all, if you can button Barbie's microscopic scoop-neck shell, you can master venal ligature as well.

Maybe, just maybe, this is all about vigilance and care, readiness to enter the fray and win the day. Maybe the Boy Scouts aren't the only guys who are always prepared.

Probably not, but maybe.

CHAPTER 7

OF GRAND CANYONS AND SMALL BONES

OR

QUIET, KIDS, I CAN'T HEAR AMERICA SINGING

As we came over the crest I shivered. There, spread out suddenly before us, was the vastness of time. The kids and I were standing on the rim of the Grand Canyon. As the purple, brown, orange, and weary light enfolded the desert, I raced through the history of Earth, imagining the modest ancient gully that gave Mother Nature this big idea. A citizen of Starship Earth, I felt quiet, alert, embedded in life, linked to any creature—coyote or cowboy—who had ever come upon this gloriousness. Then I felt a tug on my arm.

"Daddy," Josh whispered, in prelude, no doubt, to a boyish "wow." "Don't forget the quarters to make the bed shake."

He was referring, of course, to the Magik Fingers device back at base camp—the Geronimo Motel. For a mere two bits dropped into a headboard-mounted box, the chenille-covered beds would vibrate for five minutes and give the entire family a "relaxing deep-muscle massage."

Now, if you ask me, the bed didn't even move. It just buzzed and relied on the malleable minds of motel guests less skeptical than yours truly to add the shimmy. But no matter. The kids loved it. They would drop in a quarter, lie down, and start to moan with stagey pleasure, as though this was just what they needed after a hard day of being children.

By our fourth day, Magik Fingers had become our third biggest budget item, moving past sunscreen and ahead of everything save airfare and lodging. By Day Five, I'd spoken harshly to the motel desk man who'd swapped the kids eighty quarters for a twenty-dollar bill. ("I'm very sorry, sir, I meant no harm," he'd said. "It's just that making change has always been among the guest services at the Geronimo.")

Magik Fingers was all the kids could talk about. It was a quandary. I could stop the death by a thousand quarters, but then their strongest memory of the trip would be—not the soft desert air, not the smell of pine in the morning, not the $2,700 American Mom and I had sprung for, but—the forty bucks in silver at which we'd drawn the line. So we worked out a Magik Fingers compromise. In exchange for a predinner half hour of unrestricted quaking, they agreed to give me back the traveler's checks. "Okay, Dad," they had said in tandem, standing side by side, trying to look unhappy with the deal.

But now, standing with these two in the warm, dusky wind, facing a rift made of time, I wasn't inclined to be a stickler about the fine print of our agreement. "Sure, pal, I'll get the quarters," I said, barely able to control an urge to point out the transcendence with which fate had brought us face to face.

"Get ten . . . no, twelve, Dad."

"OK," said I, brother of the moon, first cousin to the crow. I felt another tug on my other side. "Daddy?" Rebecca said, about to send a startling spiritual invocation into the aether we shared with every spider that had gone before.

"Yes, doll?" I said, crouching down, squeezing her to me, trying to hug her little Navaho soul.

"Tonight, can I get the ice from the ice machine?"

In an instant my spirit fell to earth. I was a priest before an indifferent congregation. "Sure, Reb," I said, pointing hopelessly to a hawk that swooped over the chasm and then surged upward because hawks do that sort of thing in this sublime world, "You can get the ice."

As we left for the motel, I felt they had missed everything. But when I turned in at the giant wooden warrior who overlooked the parking lot, the kids gave an
Apache cheer in honor of the Geronimo, a $79.95-per-
night land of dreams. I savored the reason that they
knew nothing about time. Everybody they had ever
loved was still alive.

Traveling, setting sail, jumping off is romance itself.
Many are the poets of peregrination who have described
the invigorations of new terrain, the high adventure of
open eyes and open heart and the open road. Traveling
with children is not precisely the same thing. In fact,
it's the opposite. It's one thing to arrive in a foreign
strand burdened only with a hopeful soul, quite another to pull into Motel 6 with half your furniture and
an Airedale named Buster.

Traveling with kids is the truest test of courage.
Compared to the tollbooth tantrums parents endure,
the Oregon Trail was a shower and a shave. True, the
sodbusters, the gold diggers, the stout-hearted Swedes
and Germans and Poles who headed West in search of
a new life prevailed through flood, famine, blizzard,
sandstorm, and blight. But who among us wouldn't
rather stalk his dinner in the forest primeval than see
Chicken McNuggets turned into ammo? Who among
us wouldn't rather sleep under the vault of heaven than
under a motel blanket that's chained to a bed? Who
among us wouldn't rather see Grandma's sideboard
carried away by the wide Missouri than his underwear
in the rearview mirror?

The revelations, the raptures, the delicious despair
of traveling with kids is an epic story of motels and gas
stations, of state parks and the state police, of scenic

overlooks and everything else you've overlooked. The events and elations, strains and gains of burgers passed through slots await their chronicler, their Homer, their Gibbon. The Bruce Catton of family life knows that the real Battle of Gettysburg had nothing to do with the Civil War but took place last month at the Stuckey's just off I-80.

Offered here, in the spirit of parental solidarity, my contribution to the eventual landmark work, the testimony of a dad who has learned a few hard lessons from the heart of darkness, who has survived trips that make Hannibal's elephantine trek to Carthage look like a Sunday stroll. Here, a few lessons from the dark side of the road.

OF ZENO'S PARADOX, STATION WAGONS, AND THE DEATH OF TIME

Back in the fifth century B.C. a smart-aleck Greek philosopher named Zeno offered the world a paradox that illuminates traveling *en famille.*

An archer, he wrote, fires an arrow toward a target. After an interval, the arrow covers half the distance to the target. And after another interval, half of the half that remains. And so the arrow flies, cutting the distance to the target in half over and over again. How, Zeno asked, does the arrow ever actually reach the target, since the best it can do is constantly cut the remaining distance in half?

I don't know the answer, but five'll get you fifty that Zeno had kids. Change "target" to "Grandma's house" and "arrow" to "Toyota wagon," and the paradox makes immediate intuitive sense—at least to parents. The family wagon is exactly like Zeno's theoretical projectile. *Fact: Sure, you can get closer, but you'll never arrive.*

Among the most important facts to keep in mind is that traveling with kids isn't about distance, it's about time. A family on the road doesn't gobble up miles but time itself. Indeed, a physicist, father of three, one Henry Nass from Rutgers, came up with a bookend idea to Einstein's landmark aha that light travels at the speed limit of this particular universe. Nass's notion (which his wife has dubbed "The 'No, We're Not There Yet' Hypothesis") suggests that nothing in this universe can go any slower than a kid-packed Toyota wagon on the Garden State Parkway. According to legend, Einstein's breakthrough came when he dreamed he was riding on a beam of light. According to Nass, he wasn't dreaming when his eureka arrived; he was trying to pry Annie's sneaker out of the exact-change basket.

There's no way around it. Trips that used to take forty minutes now last through the holidays. New York to Philly used to be two hours and change. With kids, it's two days and a rest cure for the missus. Consider the following Möbius trip conversion chart, which reveals the difference in duration between identical transits—when done by adults only and when attempted with at least two representatives of the next generation.

Trips	Adults Only	With Kids
Poplar Bluffs to Little Rock	3 hours	July
Eugene, Oregon to Hope, Idaho	12 hours	What's the half-life of molybdenum?

Trips	Adults Only	With Kids
Lelanau, Michigan to Wichita Falls, Texas	3 days	Information unavailable: never completed with children
Your house to the mall	4 minutes	The time it takes for your youth to wither and die

The prechild formula for travel time is grade school stuff:

$$\frac{distance}{average\ speed}$$

But travel time with kids is:

$$\frac{infinity}{10^{-24}}$$

This is rendered for the nonscientist as "Good luck, big guy. The AAA card is in the glove box." *Fact: Families en route spend as much time standing still as they do moving toward their destination.* Consider this partial list of reasons for which I stopped the car in the period from May 1989 to February 1990:

• To retrieve Mr. Snuggles from

  1. The breakdown lane
  2. The median strip
  3. A culvert
  4. The luggage rack of the Saab with Massachusetts plates

- To buy some glue for

  1. My glasses
  2. The rearview mirror
  3. Mr. Snuggles's glasses

- To deliver a lecture on human decency
- To pry out of Rebecca's ear

  1. A raisin
  2. A dime
  3. A little Monopoly house

- To pry same out of

  1. Seat-belt buckles
  2. Mr. Snuggles's ear

- To drop Jody at the bus depot
- To report the children to the proper authorities

(Space considerations in this one-volume book do not allow inclusion of what, for purposes of delicacy, could be described as medical emergency pit stops, except to say that eight out of ten of them turn out to be neither emergent nor medical, but rather the result of psychosomatic symptoms induced by mere crankiness on the part of small people who think they're the only ones who would give anything to be anywhere but on the Dan Ryan Expressway.)

I've stopped for every conceivable reason. I've stopped four times in twelve minutes, eight times in forty-six. I've stopped for apple juice, orange juice, fruit punch, yogurt, apple juice, lollipops, raisin bread, rice cakes, and apple juice. I've made an emergency stop for crayons. Did I mention apple juice? *Fact: Given all the*

*stops, the average speed of a family journey up the
coast road is in the neighborhood of four miles per
hour.* Little wonder Tacoma seems like a dream.

Still, you've got no choice. For Mom and Dad, full
speed ahead is just not an option. I've known parents
who try to take a hard line, Chrysler K-car Mussolinis
who won't stop anywhere but the emergency room. Now
and then, they do get home before harvest. But what
price glory? The kids can't think of a car without their
stomachs hurting, and they're haunted by an image of
Mr. Snuggles orphaned under a speed-limit sign just
north of the Slauson cutoff.

Traveling with kids is especially tough on Dad, since
American men all have a gene for getting where they're
going. Fathers like to arrive. It's an atavistic holdover
from Wild West days when first guy in got to be gover-
nor. Hell, we're not even ashamed of it. Oklahomans
actually call themselves Sooners to honor the guys who
jumped the gun and bolted straight for their claim.

The plain fact is that goal orientation built this country. Try to imagine the land we'd live in today if Lewis
and Clark had dawdled at the Father Joliet Overlook.
What might have become of us if the moguls who spon-
sored and the immigrants who built the Transconti-
nental Railroad weren't antsy about a quicker trip from
Sacramento to St. Joe? Still, that was then; this is
now. There's no rush anymore. In the words of the
singing group The Eagles, parents have got to "take it
easy. Don't let the sound of your own wheels drive you
crazy."

PARENTAL TRAVEL TIPS

• Throw out your maps. If it's before noon and the
sun's on your right you're headed straight for Santa's
workshop. That's all you need to know.

• Don't even think about your actual destination, just think about the terrain that will get you there. If you're heading from Cleveland to Woonsocket, don't focus on Rhode Island but on the tumbling farmland of western New York that is your way—or is it your path? —east.

• Carry the legal limit of apple juice. Take out the spare tire and pack the wheel well with those boxes of juice that come individually wrapped with little tiny straws. The downside of a February flat on a highway outside Bozeman is no big deal compared to a drink drought on a sunny day in Palm Springs.

• Never give Aunt Nancy and Uncle Bill an even vaguely precise time of arrival. They'll only start worrying if you're a half hour late. In a perfect world you shouldn't even tell them you're coming; there's a better than even chance you'll have to turn back. But if you feel you must offer an e.t.a., choose one from the following list:

1. Thursday P.M., Friday sometime; latest, Saturday noon
2. By the next full moon
3. During the Bush administration
4. In time for the tricentennial

• Never suggest that the kids play a travel game that in any way rewards spotting license plates from various states. These games turn even nice children into liars. My friend's son claimed to have spotted cars from all fifty states, the U.S. Virgin Islands, and Guam, in the time it took his sister to reach down for a crayon. She countered by saying she had just spotted a Buick LeSabre from Jupiter.

• The night before you set out, read a few pages from one of the magnificos of travel writing—a Jan Morris or

Eric Newby—or one of the Oriental religious classics.
Life is a journey, we're all pilgrims.

TAKING THE SHOW ON THE ROAD

Despite the vexations of the road, parents have no
choice but to grab the kids and go. We've got to jump
the tracks, get to places where the light is whiter at
dawn, where the blueberries are smaller and more tart,
where the rocks are red, where the locals call it *pop*
instead of *soda*.

We've got to light out for two reasons. First, to give
the kids at least some intimation that the world is large.
And second, to reveal that the members of this team
share more than an address. I recall with the clarity of
just moments ago the nine O'Neills of my youth stream-
ing into a diner in a foreign land called Lake George. We
shaped that room with our culture as surely as we were
shaped by its sights and sounds. I remember feeling
proud of us among strangers.

You've got to go for that moment when you'll find
yourself walking toward the rim of the canyon at noon
and you'll look down at your pockets stuffed with tour-
ist brochures and then up ahead at the kids racing
away toward they know not what, and you'll feel the
muscles that link you all. There, two thousand miles
from the dailyness of kitchen and backyard, from anybody who even knows who you are, you'll revel in the
understanding that this family flows through time and
place, that forever and always, long after strangers live
at the family manse, long after you all inhabit different
time zones, you're tied together, not by the trivial bonds
of circumstance, but by the memories of Magik Fingers
that said amen to those Arizona days.

Like most travelers, you'll find things you weren't
looking for.

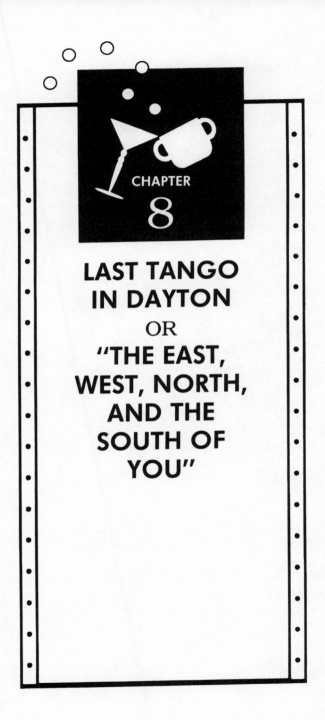

CHAPTER

8

**LAST TANGO
IN DAYTON**

OR

**"THE EAST,
WEST, NORTH,
AND THE
SOUTH OF
YOU"**

The conventional wisdom is that having children is bad news for your love life. Mom and Dad, so goes the popular myth, are more likely to be covered in oatmeal than cocoa oil. But once again, the common view is just another case of missing the doughnut that surrounds the hole.

For though it's true that parenthood does bring dramatic deprivation—mothers and fathers often have to reminisce about their sex life—that can be good news. Consider: Who is more smooch-ready than a mommy who is twenty-seven years older than anybody she spoke to all day? Who needs a cuddle more than a dad just back from a Cub Scout jamboree? Those hours with the Smurfs, those mornings of Maypo can turn Mom into a sexual desperado, Dad into a K Mart Stanley Kowalski. Struggling to be heard over the Chipmunks' greatest hits, the song of Venus becomes positively operatic. In one of life's confounding and delightful inversions, the impossibility of Mom and Dad meeting on the field of love, the long dry spells they endure together, become the very engine of romantic ingenuity.

True, your love life is changed once the kids arrive. But who among us wouldn't welcome a new wrinkle or two? There are four good reasons—three logistical, one psychological—why Mommy and Daddy get artful about their passion and become the hot stuff that dreams are made of.

Romantic Upside #1: On Your Mark, Get Set . . .
Mom and Dad can do things with, and to, each other

that civilians just can't do—or at least parents can do them more quickly. Like any successful creature, mothers and fathers adapt to their environment, which—once the kids arrive—no longer includes thirty child-free minutes. So while expressing affection used to happily take a nice langorous bite out of your evening, once you have kids, you can get where you're going in a hurry. I know a couple who claim they can be back in the living room before Cosby is back from commercial.

Romantic Upside #2: "Oh Hi, Sweetie . . ." Having kids also brings the fear of discovery back into romance. Let's face it, the possibility that any minute somebody wearing elf pajamas will appear outlined in the doorway adds a forbidden-fruit edge to cuddling. After all, where's the thrill in getting cozy if absolutely nobody is trying to stop you? Romeo and Juliet were only an item for the ages because everybody from Benvolio to Tybalt was telling them to chill out. Once you've got kids, romance is delicious brinksmanship.

Romantic Upside #3: The Basement Tapes. Kids turn your whole house into a romantic setting. Non-parents most often express affection in the bedroom. But the bedroom's not a parental option—that's the first place the kids look. Kids drive sex out of the bedroom and into the closet—and the basement, the garden, and the crawl space in the attic.

Ask a homeowner with no kids about her basement and she'll talk about mildew; ask a mommy the same question and she'll blush. Ask a father about his toolshed and he'll say his toolshed is none of your damn business. Before parenthood, couples have to deal with the tedium of those same sheets, that same wallpaper, that same ceiling, the same old noises—familiar bed springs, sighs, and cries. But after parenthood, couples arrive by Darwinian necessity in a brave new world of amorous sights, scents, and sounds. Suddenly the

backdrops of love are a Whitmanesque catalog of saw-
dust and motor oil, the shimmy of the spin cycle, the
perfume of the hydrangea bush out back. I know a couple who have a regular Friday night date on the roof,
another who use their son's treehouse more than he
does. For some, the linen closet is a honeymoon suite.
Kids turn places that used to be maintenance problems
into sweet memories.

The three-bedroom split level is no country for the
prissy. Behind the Ozzie and Harriet veneer parents
are the athletes of love, ennobling each other anywhere,
anytime, and in a manner of moments. True, they're
not much for courtly customs, the bourgeois niceties of
you-first. But who among us hasn't dreamed of a world
with fewer by-your-leaves and more here-and-now
pleas?

**Romantic Upside #4: "May I Have This Dance for
the Rest of My Life?"** Greater by far than the many
other voluptuous advantages of having children in your
house is the fact that kids turn a man and a woman
into sexual conspirators. Mom and Dad are constantly
plotting together to steal a moment of sweet abandon
from the cartoons. The intimacy of trying to satisfy
both your craving for each other and their hunger for
Froot Loops is—no other way to say it—plain old warm.

Old army buddies often report that the friendships
formed in foxholes have an inimitable intensity. With
respect for the peril of the men who fought, parenthood
is a foxhole all its own. But in the child-rearing war, the
buddy who's watching your back smells like a lily, has
hair that takes to the sunlight, and a laugh that comes
from the heart. This time you're in a foxhole with a hot
ticket, a woman whose charms the battle cannot subdue.

For the final fact is that once you have kids together
there is at last something greatly powerful between you.

Your respect and admiration, your reliance on each other, your hopefulness about this team informs, even enriches, your lust. Your hands get quiet and skilled. Your hips get smart and strong. Your hope holds softly on and, now and then, the two of you, who spend too much time mashing up peas, too much time barking that this room is a pigsty, the two of you trapped—hallelujah—for the duration, will in tandem take wing, mastering horizontal moves that would have made Fred and Ginger humble.

PARENTAL SEX CLUBS: A MODEST PROPOSAL

No question that though having kids can add an adventurous edge to sex, there will be times when Mom and Dad get nostalgic for an old-fashioned afternoon of fresh linen and each other. Don't despair. There is hope. But if parents are going to survive, we'll have to go beyond cooperation to actual cooperatives—cooperatives designed for specifically sexual purposes.

Now, this isn't near as exotic as it sounds. It doesn't include borrowing or lending spouses or any friendly group larger than a twosome. It just means that those of us with children have to help each other out. The following outlines how it might work.

For no apparent reason on a Saturday call Brenda and Jeff and ask if their kids would like to come over for the afternoon, thereby leaving B. and J. alone for a game of Scrabble.

Even if the five kids—your two, their three—do go rogue and start tearing bricks out of the fireplace, you can console yourself with three thoughts: (1) the image of Brenda and Jeff lathering each other with herbal soap in prelude, (2) the picture of same sharing Ben and Jerry's ice cream in afterglow, and (3) the delicious idea that if Brenda and Jeff are the friends you think they are, they'll come by next week and take your kids on the Fourth of July outing to the stadium.

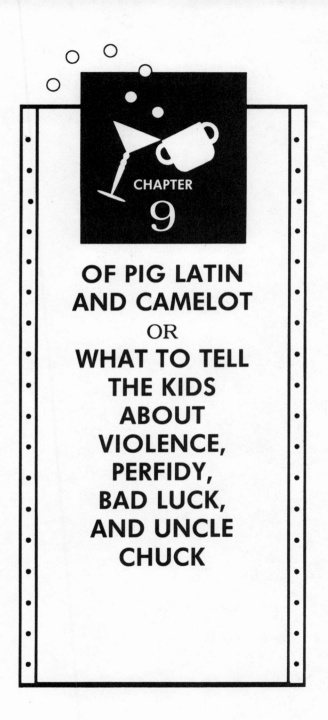

CHAPTER

9

OF PIG LATIN AND CAMELOT
OR
WHAT TO TELL THE KIDS ABOUT VIOLENCE, PERFIDY, BAD LUCK, AND UNCLE CHUCK

In the world according to Jody, Cinderella's stepmother was just having a bad day, the Big Bad Wolf threatened to huff, puff, then tickle The Three Little Pigs, and Sleeping Beauty got out of bed not because some no-account royal deigned to give her a smooch but because there was a life for a young woman to lead out there.

"But Mommy," one of the kids will say, "Jeffrey says she was wokened up when a prince kissed her on her ruby-red lips." Well, maybe next door, but not in our house she wasn't.

Jody is a motherly master at improving the world, a professional editor who blue-pencils prejudice, pestilence, plague, dissonance, divorce, death, crime, mayhem, toxic waste, and dubious taste. In the sugarcoated world according to Mommy, the Japanese were very rude to our guys at Pearl Harbor.

FRIEDMAN FAIRY TALES:
MOMMY-APPROVED VERSIONS

The Legend of Robin Hood. Robin Hood is still a fund-raiser, but no brigand. He persuades the rich to be philanthropic by explaining the joys of giving.

Jack and the Beanstalk. "Fee, fi, fo, fum, I smell the cologne of an Englishman."

Davy Crockett. Davy is born on that same mountaintop in Tennessee, but he's not much for blood sport. He does, however, *see* a bear when he is only

three and starts a local chapter of the Sierra Club to
protect creatures so grand.
Snow White and the Seven Guys. Everybody's five-
foot-six, nobody's named Dopey.

Though Jody takes it farther than most, the urge to
protect the children from the tough stuff is a parental
trademark. In the early years, we don't mention that
the history of mankind is a catalog of atrocities, but
paint the world instead as a place where probity is re-
warded, loyalty is daily bread, and affection rules the
day.

Our reluctance to tell it like it is has its adult down-
sides. To start with, it makes it nearly impossible to
have a decent conversation in front of the kids. Try
enjoying a chat that doesn't mention perfidy, betrayal,
or the triumph of the vulgar over the fine. It can't be
done; we are such stuff as schemes are made of. So we
have to bury the juicy stuff in code. Parents are expert
at the art of euphemism. We can find a toothless way to
say unimaginably shady things.

THE THREE PHASES OF DECEIVE

When the kids first arrive no camouflage is required.
Babies don't understand anything so Mom and Dad
can gab on about Steve's dalliance, Marsha's secret,
revel in the sinister side of life—the deadbeats, adul-
tery, usury, and despair. But once the children hit two
and a half or so, they start to pick up a word here and
there and parents enter . . .

The Scrabble Phase

During this phase, which usually lasts about a year,
everything gets spelled. For example:

DAD: Bad news, babe, Michael just got i-n-d-i-c-t-e-d.
MOM: For what?
DAD: L-o-a-n-s-h-a-r-k-i-n-g.
MOM: That's ridiculous, Michael's our dentist.
DAD: Tell it to the D.A.

Anything that seems unsuitable for small ears—
either bad news or just plain private—becomes part of
the National Spelling Bee. For a few months this can be
fun. Talking about mature subjects in front of the kids
has a cloak-and-dagger quality. The English language
becomes a tantalizing orthographic code that allows
you to hide in plain sight. But later this can lead to all
kinds of stress in a marriage—particularly if one part-
ner is a better speller than the other. Early in our Scrabble Phase I had to ask Jody to spell things several times.
I still claim she botches p-s-y-c-h-o-t-i-c d-e-m-e-n-t-i-a.

Much more serious, however, is the peril of a near
miss. But for a missing *s*, the *dessert* that ends dinner
is the *desert* that ends a marriage.

Still, for a time, spelling affords a measure of privacy.
But then, along comes phonics, and suddenly little
Edna is sounding out words you first learned at Fort
Ord. Suddenly spelling is no help. So, looking for other
forms of verbal flimflam, parents slide into Phase
II . . .

The Pig-Latin Interlude

There is momentary refuge in caboosing the initial con-
sonant and tacking on the old *ay* suffix.

MOM: Are you telling me our dentist is an egbreaker-
        lay?
DAD: Yup, and we're into him for an undlebay.

This can be a nice stage because pig Latin not only hides the world from the kids, but it actually softens the bad news for parents. Somehow the *ay* ending— probably because of its subliminal link to the cheerful Spanish *olé*—gives even somber words an exuberant lilt. In pig Latin, divorce—ivorce-day—sounds less like a family tragedy than it does like a Scandinavian ice festival.

Of course, pig Latin can't cover our venal tracks for long. After all, kids invented it. So some bilingual *mères* and *pères* take cover behind a second language.

Parlez-Vous Insider Trading?

For example:

> **DAD:** Michael was, *comment dit-on, un peu* drunk, last *soir*.
>
> **MOM:** *Ah oui, il* kept saying, But *je suis un* honest *homme*.

But finally, French won't give you much help in sharing your fatal visions. After all, who but the truly fluent knows the French phrase for "mass Kool-Aid suicide in the jungles of Guiana"? Further, it's not likely that the two of you speak French equally well. So, most often, instead of dishing the dirt you'll end up arguing about the use of the subjunctive.

In those early private yeasty years, we imagine we can be the authors of a generous world. But then the family castle is finally breached by the school-yard bully, and it appears, for a time, that the world will have its way with our team. Still, the tough mom and dad don't fold. They persist in smiling the edge off resentments, the blood out of war, the wicked out of witches, and the unrequited out of love. We give no glimpses into dark, grown-up hearts.

The urge to keep the hard secrets is a powerful parental inclination. My father was the very model of steadfastness. Late in his life, when an all's-well charade fell apart and it became apparent his health was failing, I chided him for not telling anybody he was sick. He looked at his thirty-five-year-old little boy in that clear-eyed way he had and said, "Son, there's only one reason I would ever give my children bad news." He paused. He smiled. He broke into his signature chuckle.

"What's that?" the son replied, a willing straight man.

"If they could possibly help," laughed the doctor who, unable to heal himself, was amused by the idea that in the final inning he would start sharing burdens with the people he had signed on to protect. Through the years, everything had been his problem. He had presided over our lives. Now, he would preside in private over his implacable death. He died with wit and grace and a mortal high style.

And now, in each daily coming-home moment, on the threshold of a home in which Hansel and Gretel get lost *with* their father, I find myself sustained, encouraged, dazzled by the high-spirited ease with which my father accomplished so august a task.

I'm not sure it's wise to protect our children so stubbornly from the bruises. Some will argue that the rub of life is best discovered a bit at a time, lest the uninitiated get ambushed. But I confess that taking the bite out of the world appeals to me. I'm flat-out for the idea of Rebecca and Josh remembering our Camelot. And if all it takes from Guinevere and me is willfulness, you'll find us the most determined stonewallers since Nixon and his less-than-merry men. We'll be the pair making ingenious excuses for everybody from Colonel Qaddafi to Captain Hook, declining even to mention those who don't share the porridge.

"Daddy," my father said to me in oblique valedictory just before he died, "is not about bad news."

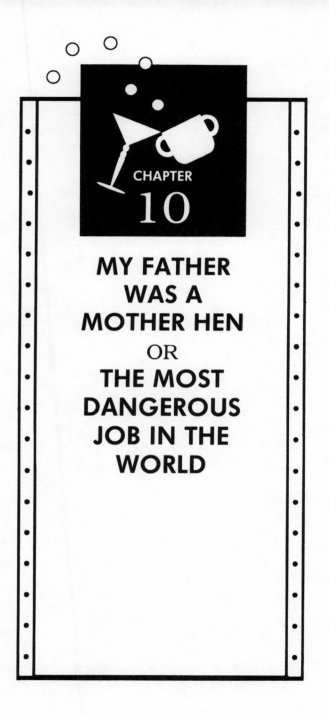

MY FATHER
WAS A
MOTHER HEN
OR
THE MOST
DANGEROUS
JOB IN THE
WORLD

Among Charles Addams's classic cartoons is a drawing that says it all about parents and the fine art of worrying. Mom and Dad are standing by their convertible on an Arizona desert road and peering, horrified, up into the sky. Exiting the panel stage right is a shadow of a humongous condor/pterodactyl with what is clearly a baseball-capped second-grader in his prehistoric claws. For parents, just when you think you've had every anxiety you can possibly have, along comes the condor/pterodactyl.

Perhaps the most dramatic change that comes with parenthood is the sudden ability to worry about practically anything. In the early days Mom and Dad look the primal illness-and-mayhem anxieties straight in the eye. But then, slowly, our self-defense mechanism subdues the unbearable concerns about health and well-being into a gentler, generalized dread that becomes the background music of being in charge of kids.

Consider just this short sampling of things parents have to sweat and to which people without kids never have to give a second thought:

- Whether the warranty covers raisins in the fuel line?
- That by the time your son is sixteen he'll know the meaning of "bench warrant," and bail will be a budget item.
- That Mednick from next door will leave work early and beat you—yet again—to *Lady and the Tramp* at the video store.

- That you'll someday pay for a wedding in which a lovely young woman will marry someone who goes by the name "Snakeman."
- That semigloss latex doesn't cover ketchup

Indeed, the parental perturbations are potent enough to reach beyond the waking hours. I have two recurring theme dreams. The first is about a daughter, grown to about sixteen, who says both of the following things:

1. "Oh, I don't know—Honduras, maybe the Yucatán?"
2. "Don't worry, Daddy, I'll call if you become a grandfather."

In the second dream, I'm on the phone with a young man, redheaded like our Josh, who starts out saying, "There's been a misunderstanding," then switches to, "No sweat, Pop, they never read me my rights," and signs off with, "Worst case, I'll cop to a misdemeanor."

No question, parents worry about it all. We worry about pesticides on fruit, about the future of the ozone layer, and the arc of tuition costs. We worry the kids will get picked last on the playground; then we worry they'll get picked first. We worry that someday they'll do mocking imitations of "Layla" by Derek and the Dominoes. We worry about tattoos, about broken bones, and broken hearts. We worry if they never eat vegetables. We worry if they ever eat candy corn. We worry the health department will get an anonymous tip about the backseat of the Chevy.

I worry about not having enough dough, about not being anything they can admire. I worry that their friends will call me Hoss. I worry that they'll make me ride the Scrambler again. I worry that I worry too much and that I won't worry enough and in an instant, one careless, could-happen-to-anybody instant, life will be changed, diminished forever. I worry that my father was right, that the world is out to get our children.

My father was a mother hen. There were seven of us chicks—Nancy, me, Kevin, Kathleen, Eileen, Tim, and Mary, in chronological order. And though it was my mother who raised us, fed us, dressed us, did the ten thousand daily chores the brood demanded, it was my father's job to worry about us. For him, it was an article of faith that life was out to get his kids, that no creatures so fine could be safe in this brutal world.

He came by his concern honestly. He was a doctor, a general practitioner with a thriving family practice in the years before that kind of doctor gave way to medical groups. And so he had a front-row seat on the carnage. He saw each of the gruesome things that couldn't possibly happen to children—except that they did. He learned to doubt the world and made it his business to warn us—about lawn mowers, about pinky rings, about diving boards, about lighter fluid, about fishhooks and rakes, about hunks of steak, about "projectiles" of all sorts, by which he meant anything that could possibly hit you in the eye, from a spitball to the Goodyear blimp. He warned us about traffic, about doors, about windows, about ice. For the third-floor bedroom he bought a great thick rope, one end of which he tied into a lasso that was to be thrown over the radiator in the event of a fire. He told us cautionary tales about broken bones, about sledding accidents. He took us to the funeral of a boy who was killed on a horse. A garrulous, affable, cheerful man, he was also a connoisseur of chaos.

Dad was ingenious in his caution. He not only

warned us about the genuine risks out there but came up with some beauts of his own devising. Often, when we were playing some harmless game or other, he would stop us to explain why we should be extra careful. Yes, we had to agree, it was not impossible to choke on a croquet mallet, and no, we'd never gone to med school and so yes, we probably were unqualified to dispute his claim that the noogie was the leading cause of coma in ten-year-olds. To my father, a jump rope was a garrote, a balloon wasn't festive but fatal; to my doctor father, a hot dog was preop to a tracheotomy.

About sleeping over at friends' houses he was a stickler. He figured it was his job to subdue intruders; he wanted his kids at home. About driving he was a master. Once we got our licenses he would invent reasons why we shouldn't drive. Statistics had proven, he would say, that there were more drunk drivers on the road on Sunday afternoon than at any other time of the week. Or perhaps it was Friday morning, or during Lent, or when it was hot, he would say, customizing his chariness to order.

But my father did lightning best of all. He was its poet laureate. He could worry about a good bolt in the basement on a clear day. At the first drop of rain, we were not only to come inside but we were to stay away from windows as well. According to my father, no prudent person even took a shower when it was raining. Once, when my brother Kevin and I were teenagers, my father drove his car across a golf course and scooped us up from the fourteenth green. We thought Mom had died; he had heard a weather report about scattered showers due that afternoon.

There was just one glorious exception to Dad's sentry duty. By some miracle Kevin and I found ourselves actually sitting around a camp fire at night with other Boy Scouts. Apparently we were going to sleep outside, where lightning had the home-field advantage. No-neck Brennan teased us about being allowed out: "Whatsa matter? Your old man croak or somethin'?" Dad was famous. We couldn't believe we were in the woods at midnight. Crackle and wood smoke and glow, it was a night for a band of boys.

But then, suddenly, carried on the wind through the pine and birch, came a faint but unmistakable sound. "Hugh-ie, Kev-in." I looked across the flames at Kev. "Don't panic, he'll never find us," Kevin's eyes said. "It's midnight and we're three miles deep in the woods." But closer and closer the sound came. "Hugh-ie, Kev-in." This time Rusty heard it too. So did Mr. Reilly, the scoutmaster. The echo of breaking brush snapped through the night.

Kevin and I stood up to gather our packs and sleeping bags. I felt a few drops of rain and knew that Dad was on lightning watch. He emerged into the clearing wearing a gray suit, paisley tie, and wing-tip shoes, Natty Bumpo by way of Brooks Brothers. He said nothing but turned to Mr. Reilly and snapped off a salute. "No disrespect intended, sir," it said, "but I need these men for another mission." It was a gesture of some grace. One thing was clear, we were on Dad's mind. He was standing guard.

Before my kids were born, the world seemed a safe place. Since my father died, it has seemed full of peril.

There is a dreary wisdom that sees courage in physical daring—thrill seekers who drive fast, court danger under a hang glider. James Dean had a self-destructive allure; a father in the produce section does not. But the truth is that compared to parenthood, the north face is horizontal.

Having a child is not just stepping into the ring with Mike Tyson, but jutting out your chin and taunting the champ. Twenty-four hours a day Mom and Dad are just asking for it. We live under the shadow of the hammer, the roundhouse right, the haymaker, lights out. Keeps a fellow light on his feet.

CHAPTER

11

**THANKS FOR
EVERYTHING,
BIG GUY**
OR
**OF MICKEY
MOUSE
PANTIES AND A
SKATING DUCK**

I am a man of few complaints. I see a glass as half full as long as it's anywhere near the fridge. But there is one thing about children that vexes even this sunny-side-up father. *Fact: Kids are just not good at gratitude—never have been, never will be.* The whole concept eludes them. King Lear summed it up when he learned of his daughters' plan to divvy up his kingdom just a tad *before* he died. "How sharper than a serpent's tooth," said the royal dad, "to have a thankless child."

Consider two stories—one concerning Disney panties, the other a Donald Duck extravaganza—with a common chord. They are offered here not because anyone doubts that kids are major-league ungrateful, but simply because it would help me to talk about them.

OF BIKINIS AND THE BABE

I was cruising through Caldor when they caught my eye—Mickey Mouse panties, three for $2.99, the last bargain on planet Earth. No question, Reba would flat love them. Panties were her life. Pink, blue, flowered, a Spiderman pair handed down from Josh, she loved them all. With the possible exception of Mickey and Minnie Mouse, Reb dug nothing more than a good chat about panties. Anyway, the question wasn't whether to buy the panties, but how many I could carry.

While driving home I tried to imagine the feeling of having your two favorite things in life combined. When I handed her the package wordlessly—no need to paint the lily—she didn't disappoint. She looked at it for a beat, then said, "Daddy, these are panties," as though I couldn't possibly have understood the vastness of what I had done. Then, when she realized they also bore the image of the trademarked Feral One, she whispered as though in church, "Daddy, these are panties with Mickey Mouse on the panties." Reader, she started to dance.

Now this should be a happy story, yes? For $2.99 Dad's a hero and the girl-child sees the world as a magical mystery tour. Wrong. From that day forward, she who had been the very model of permissive panty-wearing, wouldn't even consider donning a pair of Mickey-less briefs. Every time Jody or I reached an undie-seeking hand hurriedly into a drawer and pulled out a plum- or peach- or apricot-colored pair she had, just days ago, worn with brio, Reba would lie rigidly down on the floor, cross her arms over her body, and declare, "I want the Mickey panties."

Of course, where the teensy-weensy Mickey panties were in the Augean pile of laundry that on occasion threatened to swallow our home, only God could even guess. I would bend over this tiny, not-entirely-nonviolent resister and try to explain the logistics of kid clothes. "Reba, you don't understand. No parent can actually *find* the Mickey panties. They just now and then appear. That's how we know it's time to wear them." But it was to no avail; Reba didn't negotiate.

Simple parental truth: No good deed goes unpunished. If the panty episode didn't prove the peril of doing something nice, there was nowhere to hide after the day . . .

OF MICE ON ICE

A trip to Radio City Music Hall, landmark home of the Rockettes. Big day out. Family adventure, four tickets to "Disney on Ice"—Mickey, Goofy, Dumbo, et al., on skates. Inside, the just-perfect clamor and glamour of the grand old building. Children and parents—alert, alive, prepared for pleasure.

We ponied up for a few trademarked trinkets—one Glowing Dragonmaster Sword, one Mickey painter's cap, splashed à la Pollock—and made our way to seats hard by the stage. When Gepetto's boy Pinocchio stopped *en pointe*, he showered us with a Sonja Henie spray. Mother and Father imagined the great hall as a sliver of their kids' ancestral memory; the kids were astonished that Donald was such a good skater.

Five minutes.

Then ten minutes.

Then fifteen minutes of theatrical wonder.

Then it happened. Then came the first hint of a serpent in the family garden.

We noticed two official-looking usher types beckoning children out of their seats and escorting them up toward the stage. The kids, maybe two dozen of them, were wearing gypsylike scarves emblazoned with The Three Little Pigs. In an instant, Jody and I knew these kids were going up on stage. They wouldn't—like our underprivileged pair—be mere witnesses, bystanders, but they would actually become chorus-line colleagues of Pluto. They were actually going to *visit* the Magic Kingdom. Jody looked at me, her face a tragic mask.

She tripped an usher and offered him a thousand dollars to include Rebecca and Josh in the Von Disney Family Singers. No dice. Five hundred dollars for two scarves, she countered. Nothing doing. She'd found the last honest man in America,.

We could only pray. We could only hope that our kids—along with three thousand others who would turn on their parents in an instant—wouldn't notice that they were having a far less exciting time than the two dozen sycophants who had arrived early and gotten the complimentary neckware.

"Daddy?" Josh said nervously. "Those kids aren't going to be in the show, are they?" He was hoping that they'd been gathered together to be punished for wearing those silly scarves. But in his heart he knew what for a moment his brain wouldn't accept—that once again Mommy and Daddy had blown it. Those other kids were going to ride in the ice trolley, he wasn't, and life—despite the Glowing Dragonmaster Sword, nay, perhaps even because of the enormous promise it had held so short a time ago—tasted now, and probably forever, like ashes.

"I'm not sure, Joshie," I said, as if maybe the kids were part of an underage work crew that was going to clean up the ice shavings.

"But what do you *think*, Daddy?" he continued, a sarcastic district attorney.

"I think they have to go up on that slippery ice, Joshie. But they'll probably be OK," I said, the voice of reassurance.

"Can I go, Daddy?"

"Oh no, don't worry, pal. You don't have to go." He was silent for an instant as his face turned into an emblem of disaster. Then he started to cry, a keening, mournful wail that—enriched by the simultaneous lament of thousands—ascended wavelike in a whining cascade through the vaulted arch. From over my shoulder to my left I heard a six-year-old reward his father for a big day out with an unforgettable snarl of kid sarcasm, "Thanks a lot, Dad."

I turned around and tried to wordlessly convey my solidarity with the perfectly nice man who was the target of the missile. When he nodded back in appreciation, I thought to myself that, as kids went, King Lear's girls weren't so bad.

None of this is a real knock on the kids. After all, they're trapped by their wide horizons. The bounce of youth makes it tough to see how hard Mom and Dad are working. The kids can't possibly know that the daddy who told the story of the brave little butterfly ten—I swear, ten—times isn't a rat for stopping at ten, but a saint for getting past three. They can't know that the family weekend in Gettysburg took more planning than the Civil War itself.

Still, this doesn't stop me from an occasional paternal fantasy of acknowledgment. I had a dream once in which the kids handed me a handsomely wrapped bottle of cognac with a crayoned note that read, "To Dad, with thanks for the reading, the wrestling . . . well, with thanks for everything, big guy."

Of course, at end of day, I'm not even sure I want the kids to be grateful for Jody and me. They might as well appreciate gravity. There's something wrong with a six-year-old being grateful for dinner. After all, to appreciate anything you've got to know something about loss, about how hard the world is on beauty and kindness and good humor. To appreciate anything, you've got to know that bodies get tired and hearts get weary.

Sometimes, standing over them while they're sleeping, I find myself happy, maybe even a little proud, that they are oblivious to their blessings. I find myself grateful enough for all of us, grateful first, that the world—so brutal, so full of blight and bad luck—has allowed them to thrive until now, and second, that they are finally—hallelujah—asleep.

TWO, FOUR, SIX, EIGHT . . . WHO SHOULD THEY APPRECIATE?

I don't doubt that the thanklessness of the kids is some kind of generational payback for the way we treated our parents. But I am nonetheless not convinced we should just endure it stoically. Unless the kids know what a privilege it is to live in this particular family they can't possibly grow up feeling as blessed as they deserve to feel.

Of course, I understand that we don't have many options. I once started telling my kids how grateful they should be for everything they had and I ended up re-counting an Abe Lincolnesque tale about how I used to walk three miles to school with no shoes, and about my cousin, Huck, who had to share the family trousers with his sister, Little Eva. I understand that there's no percentage in "Do you know how lucky you are to have a mother like Mommy?" From that comes a memoir that will make little Philly Roth's meditation on Mom read like a valentine.

But there are a few little subliminal tricks that can plant a count-your-blessings seed. Go for the gratitude. Consider the following opportunities.

A, B, C, D . . . I Love Dad. All children are sur-rounded by the letters of the alphabet—on blocks, in puzzle form, those magnetic letters that clutter the fridge. But most often, the letters are just wasted, tossed carelessly about in phonetic jumbles, spelling out words like LMLEZ.

Whenever possible, try arranging the letters in purposeful messages for the kids. I once spelled out the following message on the dinosaur bookcase that I spent seven days building and that they never once, not once, mentioned: "Isn't it lucky that Dad has enough skill and enough love to work so hard on this?" True, it cost me forty dollars in magnetic letter sets, but when Josh came up to me and said, "Hey, Dad, thanks for the bookcase," believe me, it was worth it.

Of Charles Dickens and Hansel's Dad. Another way to prod their grateful gland is to be sure to read them books that only feature wretched parents. Hansel and Gretel's dad—you know, the guy who left his kids alone in the woods because the new wife thought they were a drag—is enough to make your kids get a mite covetous about you. Cinderella's stepmom will make you look like a box of chocolates.

Though Dickens on the printed page is a reach until at least the teen years, the original movie version of *Oliver Twist* makes it pretty clear that even being stuck with Mom and Dad is a step up from the underworld of London, to which kids without parents are doomed.

Finally, almost anything written by Roald Dahl (with the luminous exception of the sweetest father-son story ever written, *Danny, The Champion of the World*) stars parents or parent-surrogates so rotten that your kids will be reminding you that yogurt is loaded with cholesterol.

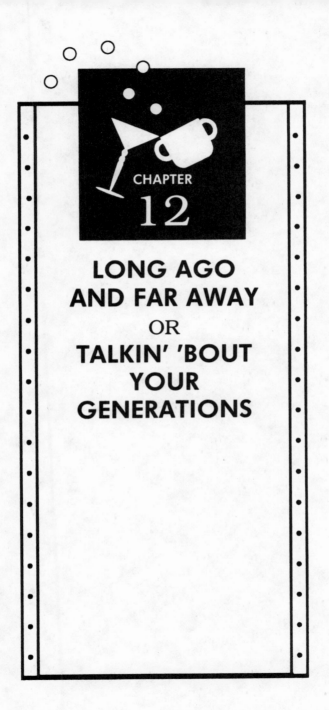

CHAPTER

12

LONG AGO
AND FAR AWAY
OR
TALKIN' 'BOUT
YOUR
GENERATIONS

All the best romances are about a distant time, when the world was more responsive to valor. And so, parents are obliged to propagate the legend of previous generations.

This is but a deeper chord of the origin myth, discussed earlier, concerning the legend of Mom and Dad's first meeting. Now with luck—assuming your forebears weren't all gangsters—it won't call for out-and-out mythmaking. It will for certain, however, require that you look back without grievance, with a weakness at least, an enthusiasm if at all possible, for the people from whom you sprang. If Uncle Ben was a less than great man, the stories of his way with a pool cue add, if little else, some color to the family shield.

If sentiment about those that went before is not your strong suit, here are two pieces of kid culture—one song and one movie—that will help put you in the mood.

OF COUSIN TOM AND FAMILY TREES

Tom Chapin is a rawboned, open-faced troubadour of childhood. His songs mix the goofy gags of youth with a hearty manliness quite remarkable in songs about lollipops and snowmen. In particular, his signature tune, "Family Tree," is a potent encomium to relatives, ancestors, and world geography.

We're a family and we're a tree.
Our roots go deep down in history.
From my great-great-granddaddy reaching up to me,
We're a green and growing family.

The singular achievement of this song isn't the ingenious internal rhyme or the Whitmanesque command of place names, but that it somehow sells both the eccentric legend of just us and the equally romantic idea that tribal instincts are the enemy, that everybody's in this together. We're talking here about both your family and the family of man. If this goes against your political grain, get yourself a new political grain.

Trust me, the melody is up to the lyrics. Make this your family anthem.

OF NANNY HARAN AND FIEVEL MOUSKEWITZ

While it's no doubt true that the glory days of animated feature films are gone, Don Bluth's *An American Tail* is a vigorous exception.

The Mouskewitz family flees the marauding feline Cossacks of Russia in favor of America, the golden cat-free land where the streets are paved with cheese. During the passage, young Fievel is swept overboard. He washes ashore on the island where the Statue of Liberty is being built by a French pigeon/architect (think Maurice Chevalier in *Gigi*.) After lamenting that America is too big for him to ever find his family, he is emboldened by a rousing duet rendition of "Never Say 'Never' Again."

On several occasions, he comes within a whisker of stumbling upon Mama, Papa, and sister Tilly in the huddled masses of New York's lower east side. Climax in a happy reunion when Fievel recognizes the sound of his father's violin through the roistering hubbub of Olde New York.

This movie will be especially resonant to parents who come from recent immigrant stock, Russian Jews in particular. Though it does have a more than occasional ethnic stereotype—including a devil's rendition of Irish mice—its spirit is euphoric and upbeat, wide-eyed about the homely glamour of our history.

Of course, any Mom and Dad who would peddle our progenitors has not only to blend the past and the present, but two separate source legends—Mom's and Dad's—as well. It's a tricky business—ransacking two mature cultures in favor of one with a best-of-both-breeds vigor. But just as the kids are entitled to the toughest genes, so are they deserving of the most potent myths from Mom's people and Dad's.

GETTING BIGGER THROUGH HYBRID VIGOR
OR
THE TRUE LAWS OF IN-LAWS

In-lawdom is no country for the faint of heart. Consider that shortly after their marriage, Romeo and Juliet, rather than dealing with the stress of the Montague–Capulet Easter supper, opted to eat poison and die. For some reason the in-law link is a low-context bond, without models in fiction or film. Ever read a novel about a boy and his father-in-law?

The in-law bond can be more than stand-up comedians. The trick is an ambidextrous legend, an understanding that the vital lies on which your in-laws rely are every bit as harmless as those your family came to cherish years ago. The notion that Aunt Julie has a beautiful singing voice, that corporate life is a vulgarity or, conversely, that life outside a corporation is just kidding around, that all Republicans suffer from sexual deprivation, that chicken salad is properly made with walnuts, not grapes, are no sillier than the things your half of your team believes. They're just more obvious. They are also, taken together, the liturgy of the tribe that produced the woman who is your best hope.

Deferring to your in-laws' legend means finding out where their people come from, caring about whether the accordion is a centuries-old or rather a more recent family tradition. It means liking their jokes. It means getting over the notion that accidental bonds of blood are somehow more serious than dedications we choose. It means instructing your affections. It means that a family begins with a simple decision to be devoted, a willingness of the heart.

When the kids arrive do at least these three things:

- Give them names that honor both legends. For example: Joshua O'Neill.
- When standing next to your father-in-law, looking through the nursery window at his new grandson, say that you think this two-minute-old sparrow looks like his brother, Frank, the guy with the thick neck. It is, of course, a ridiculous thing to say but, he'll know what you mean.
- Tell the kids about both your parents and Mom's. If your mother-in-law makes the best cookies in West Virginia or the best laws in Utah, pass this stuff on to your five-year-old. Make your mate's people much-storied.

After all, there's not a family in the world—including the one you came from and the one you aspire to oversee—that isn't full of oddness. Figuring that out takes neither brains nor character, just an attitude.

But figuring out what's grand about these people, figuring out how they brought this true love of yours to such invigorating term, that's worth your energy.

There is a lesson in the ninety-four-year-old grandmother-in-law who remembers everything her granddaughter's husband has ever told her about any one of his four sisters and two brothers, three brothers-in-law, two sisters by marriage, and six nieces. And an instructive tale is told of a legendary Jewish mother-in-law and father-in-law who, on the occasion of their daughter's wedding to an Irish-American Catholic, prepared a wedding tape on which Hebrew and Gaelic sounds took turns and harmonized.

ON PHOTOGRAPHS OF DISTANT MEN

Romance is hope. It requires a distrust of the rational mind, a pledge of unreasonable allegiance. It requires a good deal of respect, a generous imagination, no small stroke of luck, and a voluptuous attachment to your history. Nobody does it better than Judith Stalberg Friedman, mother of my wife, grandmother to my kids, the keeper of the Stalberg-Friedman and now-O'Neill flame.

She has raised the family photograph to the level of art. Her home is the work of a world-class curator. On every surface, in antique frames culled from second-hand shops, she displays in stop-action the saga of her crowd. It's all there watching over today—the haughty hopeful faces and high collars of Russians in a new land, an American boy, her son, with tricycle and stripes, the seven-year-old Annie Oakley who would grow into Jody, friends getting older and wiser and older as the years gave way. There, in time lapse, is an assertion that we matter, a context for our days.

And everywhere there are pictures of her father—in voluble midsentence, in contemplative midthought, at thirty-six in the full power of young manhood, at sixty, gray and vivid, face full of laughter and sweetness and woe. I find myself telling Josh and Reb tales of his life and times. Thanks to his daughter and to hers, he is the Stalberg-Friedman version of Merlin, whose readiness for the world continues, twenty-five years after his death and for a grandson-in-law he never met, to make everything seem both heartbreaking and just fine.

CHAPTER

13

HUSH LITTLE DADDY, DON'T SAY A WORD

Night and day, we never sleep
The kids at 2 in the morn into our
    bed will creep
When their feet are at your throat
And your head is on a plastic boat
You'll be awake
Night and day . . .
        —with apologies to Cole Porter

Though the middle-of-the-night shenanigans of newborns are infamous, it's less well-known that parental sleep deprivation doesn't pass with infancy. A Tom Cheney cartoon best describes the tenure of parental sleep shock: A mustachioed thirty-nine-year-old son in striped pajamas is standing, entreaty in his eyes, in the doorway of Mom and Dad's room. Elderly Dad, from a sleeping position cuddled up next to antique Mom, says, "Son, your mother and I think you're old enough to get your own glass of water."

The lack of sleep that comes with kids is a done deal. Whether you're awakened by another report of the growly monster in the closet or you just bolt awake from a dream about the tuition monster, you're getting up, pal. The only open question is how to handle it, how to feel about the fact that you're going to stagger through your life wondering if you might catch a quick nap in the crosswalk.

There are two choices: (1) You can gripe in the full knowledge that you're entitled, or (2) you can do what I decided to do when I heard myself explaining to the cashier at Wendy's that no, I hadn't had a stroke, I was just a bit overtired. You can choose to revel in sleeplessness, consider it a doorway to a dark, nocturnal, and exotic realm, a land beyond the feckless light of day. You can resent and lament the kids' early-morning high crimes. Or you can jump the conformist high-noon tracks of your life and prowl a gray-white world of visions and dreams. It's your call—you can whimper that somebody stole your pillow, or you can get like Baudelaire.

Energy spent actually trying to get some sleep is wasted; it won't happen. Your best hope is ingenuity used to beatify your fatigue. To that end here are a few instructive memories of wee-hour atrocities, a scientific riff on the perils of dreams deferred and a preposterous celebration of the joys of staying awake forever.

OF MUSICAL BEDS AND THE GIRL I WED

I'm not convinced Freud was right about the Oedipus complex, that we all, at some level, want to get physical with Mom. But experience has taught me one thing—everybody wants to sleep *next* to her. In my house the hours between midnight and 7 A.M. are a pitched battle, a steel-cage wrestling match for the spot next to Jody, who, if I'm not mistaken, was my wife long before she was anybody's mother. Though the following log dates from shortly before Rebecca's third birthday, it could describe almost any night before or since.

1 A.M.: Josh wakes me and looms over me, a drowsy wraith in Roger Rabbit pajamas. "I wanna cuddle with Mommy," he moans in prelude to another story about the famous burglar who apparently swings past his window every night. This plundering Tarzan "wears a mask like a raccoon face, Dad."

"Back in your bed, pal," I say as I guide him back to the nifty little boy's bed we paid American cash for him to sleep in. "This is your bed," I add with a flourish. "It's that simple, Josh. Good night." And so, back to bed with Jody, my wife.

1:40 A.M.: Rebecca arrives at my bedside. She's typically naked and nervy. "Move over," she'll command. "Make some room next to Mom."

"No way, kiddo," I counter. "You have a bed. You cannot sleep with me and Mommy."

"I don't want to sleep with you," says she, "I just want to sleep with Mommy." OK, I think, point made and point taken.

"Nope, here's your bed," I'll say, pointing to the cozy doll-choked chaos, firmly marking the limits that every child-rearing professional in the world agrees kids not only need but actually want, though the screaming and crying can be misleading.

1:42 A.M.: I stumble back to our bed and find Josh, who has reclaimed what I like to think of as my spot. He expects me to believe—in spite of the smile on his face—that he is in a comatose slumber.

Words won't move him. So, I bend over, planning to lift him up. But since he's now the size of a small woman, I end up half-dragging him down the hall to his room. As we're about to thwomp over the door jamb to his room, he wakes up suddenly and launches into some ACLU-inspired spiel about the right way and the wrong way to remove nonviolent resisters. He points to his ear and claims I nearly tore it off his head.

"Is it still attached, Dad?" he whimpers.

"Go to sleep, Josh," I beg, "If you have the smallest shred of love for me, please, my son, go to sleep."

"Oh sure," he says, showcasing his six-year-old sarcasm, "I love you, Dad, but I also loved my ear."

1:45 A.M.:   Back once more to Jody and guess who? Rebecca, a buck-naked starfish, splayed out in the center of the bed, her left pinky in Jody's right eye. She is now wearing a tyrannosaurus backpack.

Guarding my marital bed I'm an NHL highlight film, a goalie in boxer shorts—diving, flopping, flailing my arms and legs as the kids hurl themselves, over and over again, pucklike, toward the goal (i.e., Mom). But what can one man do facing two hundred kamikaze children who've turned themselves into human projectiles? I fight the good fight for a time, but most often I'm forced to take my pillow and hit the road.

During my exiles I wander through the house in a

stupor—awake but insensate, lobotomized by fatigue. Driven by my id, I might well wolf down six or a hundred cookies. I might watch volleyball from Japan or flip idly through the phone book thinking there was somebody I wanted to call. Jody claims—and I have no reason to doubt her—that she once came upon me at dawn speaking in tongues to a bowl of Mallomars. I was a barbarian, a subhuman zombie, psychologically undone by sleep deprivation.

Once I become an exile, where I'll end up is anybody's guess. Over the last eighteen months I've slept:

- In all the beds
- Under two of them
- On both couches
- Behind one of them
- In the car
- In my neighbor's car
- In my neighbor's garage
- With my neighbor's wife (inadvertent)
- Seated at/on top of/under my desk
- On the basement stairs
- In the tub
- On the lawn chaise out back
- Guarding the driveway

It's also a dice roll as to what I'll end up under. I have awakened cozied under these and other makeshift blankets:

- The business section of the *New York Times*
- The kids' pup tent
- A Hefty handle-tie trash bag
- The slipcovers from the love seat
- Six pairs of sweat socks and a dicky

And I've used as a pillow each of the following items:

- A penny loafer (Sebago, cordovan)
- A barrel of Tinkertoys
- The Random House Dictionary of the English Language
- The keyboard of an Apple II
- A pencil
- The bottom drawer of the dresser
- The flipped-open lower door to the oven
- Two pot holders

The pot holders weren't the least comfortable, but I smelled like gravy till noon. A beagle followed me to work.

These sojourns are a physical ordeal, to be sure. But given the scientific facts about sleep—or more specifically, dreams—the corporal consequences are tame compared to the psychological assault.

ON DAD AND DREAMS DEFERRED

Humans, and that includes parents, dream during what is called the REM (rapid eye movement) stage of sleep. You pass through it once on the way down to the restful regions and once more as your body eases back to consciousness. It is the time when your subconscious expresses itself in dreams which, and here Freud can be trusted, are mental hygiene, nature's way of untying a few psychic knots.

Parents face a particular biopsychological threat. Because they're rousted every nine minutes they never sink beneath the REM stage. So, not only do they get too little rest, their few moments of repose are a perpetual dream state, a psychological surge and overload.

Now, in their natural small doses, bookending a nice eight hours, dreams may well be the release valve Freud imagined. But a steady diet of surreal scenarios is enough to push even the most well-adjusted mom or dad over the edge. It's pretty tough to winnow the mayhem from your mind when every sleeping moment is a loop of domineering women who look like Sister Francine and are wearing nothing but leather aprons and nurse hats.

For a time in 1987 I thought I would unravel. The physical deprivation brought me near the edge. Like a marathon runner I had hit the wall. I would either collapse in a heap or break through to some inner reserves. And then late one night, munching on some graham crackers and mustard, I saw the light through the good offices of a TV evangelist with the worst toupee in the world I saw the light. "If life gives you lemons," he said, as though he were the first guy to say it, and moving his hair left, "make lemonade." My choice was clear—I could come undone, go for a state cholesterol record, or I could make lemonade, give myself over to the lessons of the night.

And with that simple epiphany I saw through the conventional daytime well-mannered empty suit I had been. And I began to cultivate a self-image bolder than a drowsy parent. I was a wild-eyed poet of the moon, half-brother to Rimbaud, a weary and sinister priest of early A.M. And if, on occasion, I crawled, sleep-starved, under a table, so be it. I would know two things that the mere sleepers of the world did not: (1) that the table was made in Hong Kong and (2) that the left trestle was two inches off center. And if I slept every Sunday in the tub, well, then I would know the pristine chill of porcelain against my manly flank. What cared I if I wasn't tucked safely into bed like all the scriveners of the world?

One way or another, the kids get you to new places.

CUDDLE UP A LITTLE CLOSER

Bedtime is Waterloo, Mom and Dad are all in, desperate for a rest. But nobody whose job it is to be tired is the slightest bit sleepy. So there can be a lot of whining and barking. Phrases like "Get in bed" and "But, Daddy . . ." can write a crabby coda to an otherwise sunny day.

And though there is no doubt in my mind that a ruthless drill-instructor observance of rules is best for all concerned, I oftentimes find myself giving in to temptation and agreeing to cuddle with the kids. Make no mistake. This is not because I'm a generous father; no, it's because I'm addicted to the moment just beyond the day and before sweet dreams.

It arrives without warning, the moment of surrender. Sometimes thirty seconds after they've thrown *Horton Hears a Who* in a rage, you can feel the little body go limp as they surrender to the inevitable, give themselves over to sleep. In that capitulation they speak with a sweet and secret clarity, without the hesitation that marks the public voice. Sometimes, Becky's murmurs seem a summons from a farther place. Sometimes, I imagine that this is no longer rehearsal, that my life has, at last, arrived and it's wearing Spiderman pajamas.

I know they should get in bed, pull up the covers, get kissed on the brow, and go to sleep. I know. I know if you lie down with them now, it will only guarantee that they'll never, God help them, be able to sleep alone. I know if I cuddle up in search of that quietness I'll wake up in my gray chalk-stripe suit wondering for an instant where I am. Still, I recommend the moments just before the kids give way to sleep, when the unmistakable swoon of their muscles and the steady rales of their breath announce that all shall be well.

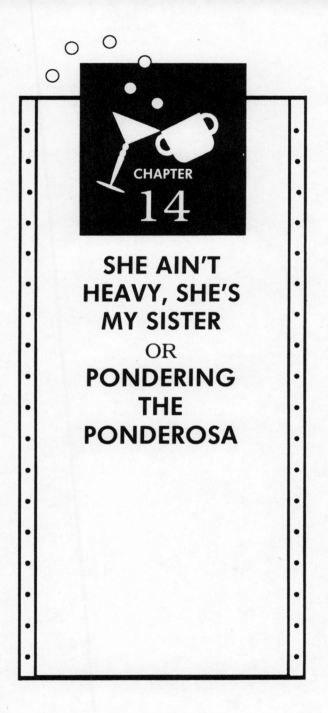

CHAPTER

14

SHE AIN'T HEAVY, SHE'S MY SISTER

OR

PONDERING THE PONDEROSA

Ben Cartwright is my guiding star.

Back in the mid-1960s, NBC's long-running television hit "Bonanza" was an O'Neill family ritual. Every Sunday, our gang would gather around Dad in his recliner to watch the single-parent Ponderosa adventures of Ben and his sons—the brainy Adam, the huge Hoss, and the mercurial Little Joe. Come what may—rustlers, drought, a gunfighter, yet another wife for Ben—the moral of the story was always loyalty. The Cartwrights stood by each other. 'Nuf said.

Now, twenty-five years later, I have dedicated myself to a Ben Cartwright cult of family loyalty. I've made it my business to promote the idea of the O'Neill-Friedmans as the end-of-millennium Cartwrights, not so much a family as the embodiment of teamwork, devotion, and dedication.

There are those who think it's ridiculous to run your family in imitation of a TV show. I'm thinking of one person in particular who thinks Rebecca and Josh should be left alone to *discover* the sinew of family, instead of being "brainwashed" with dimly remembered summaries of television scripts about the Nevada territory. She thinks as well that only a "nut" writes a family musical called *Let's Have Zeal for Team O'Neill*. Apparently, she also thinks that when your lyricist-husband chirps, "Everything rhymes with O'Neill," it's funny to respond, "Yeah, including *congeal*."

I have been guilty of excess. I did once suggest that maybe instead of complaining that Rebecca hit him in

the head with an ice-cream scooper, Josh might thank
God he's got a sister. But Jody doesn't understand that
all extravagantly successful teams—from the unlikely
Mets of '69 to the corporate cohort at IBM—rely on slo-
gans to propagate the mandate. I make no apology for
inventing the family cheers.

Mom and Dad have to do some selling. They can't
leave the loyalty lessons to nature. Adam and Eve did,
and their boys took a game of "Gotcha last" one step
over the line. Parental blandishments on behalf of the
team are a necessary antidote to the biological rub of
kids who argue over the proper sequence of the seasons. (The girl-child insists there's a season called
"snow.")

Now, I will admit that right now it's tough to see the
results of my salesmanship. Indeed most often the kids
turn my weakness for us against me. When Rebecca
was trying to sell me on the importance of having
Cherry Merry Muffin's Kitchen Set in our home she
said, "Dad, I was just thinking how much I love Josh."
And I sometimes think that "Family, schmamily" is
Josh's favorite expression. At moments like these, Jody
will look at me as though they somehow prove that I'm
overselling.

But what certain people don't understand is that I'm
not playing for the short-run victory. These early years
are a one-time window of opportunity. All my slogan-
eering about the O'Neill-Friedman team is a hedge
against the future, that implacable tomorrow when
they're grown and our family—so monolithic now—will
seem like a paltry slice of the versatile wide world. My
hope is that after centrifugal force sends them out there
in search of more, the memory of the handy-dandy bro-
mides of a Ben Cartwright apostle will burble up
through the complexity and sustain them through the
indifference of anybody who's not us.

My hunch is that though from the middle of the muddle my enthusiasm may seem, in Jody's phrase, "too much," it may, when retrieved in tranquillity, seem encouraging and sweet. Family, like any language, is best learned when young. As long as the kids learn its grammar now, they can get sincere about it later.

Sometimes when we hear the kids sharing one of those spring-fed chuckles from a farther room, or when they parade into our bedroom, banging together sneakers and singing "Frère Jacques" in some kind of Valentine's Day parade, or when we come across them dancing, cheek to chest, in front of the fridge, I'll look over at Jody and, somehow, *not* say "I told you so."

"Excuse me, Hugh?" she'll ask, in response to nothing, just a trace of threat in her voice.

I'll say nothing again.

Then she'll counter with—and here, to my mind, the lady doth protest too much—"This has nothing to do with your DNA dance number, you know."

"Of course not, doll," I'll respond with dazzling insincerity.

In those moments I allow myself to savor their future together. I imagine them all grown, sharing elations, letdowns, an occasional dim memory of Mom and effusive remembrance of me. I imagine that they'll raise families in houses side by side, that they'll teach each other, lend each other dough before they have to ask, and love each other's children. Mostly, I imagine that whenever Josh walks into the saloon in Virginia City and sees Rebecca getting thwumped over the head with some furniture, he won't ask questions about what mule-headed thing his sister did to start the fracas, but just wade in and start swinging.

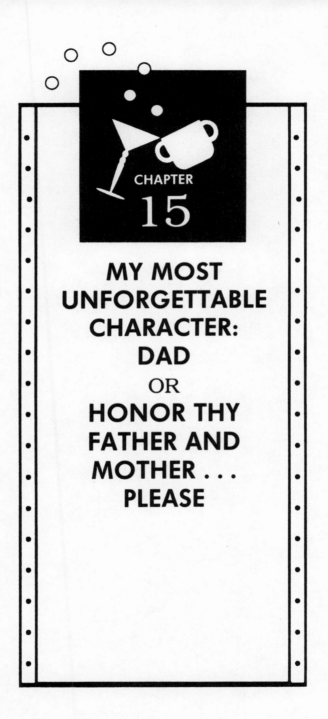

CHAPTER

15

MY MOST
UNFORGETTABLE
CHARACTER:
DAD
OR
HONOR THY
FATHER AND
MOTHER . . .
PLEASE

I often wonder what my kids see when they look at me. I have a strong hunch that, even if the kids knew who Winston Churchill was, my signature phrase "Enough already, go to bed" would not bring The Great Lion to mind. But I aspire nonetheless to be someone worth looking at, to be a model of everything from good manners to good faith, to combine all those opposites—gentleness and strength, seriousness and mirth—into an approximation of a grown-up.

I confess: I want my kids to admire me without measure. At least for the early years, I'd like them to think of their dad as a singular fellow, a man among men, a brave, thrifty, reverent spirit prone to loyalty and laughter. In short, a better guy than Philip's dad, next door. This is not the same hunger for adulation that has driven dictators since Day One. No, I just want my kids to feel as safe as I felt.

But the truth is that parenthood throws a spotlight on your shortcomings not your virtues.

There are those who argue that having children is little more than a biological ego trip. And I suppose there is some creature kick in seeing your genetic legend caper across the lawn. But for my money, bottom-line, parenthood is pretty tough on the old self-esteem. Frank Capra's *It's a Wonderful Life* has a throwaway line that tells: "Hey, Dad," asks Jimmy Stewart's oldest boy, "how do you spell *frankincense?*"

Kids blow your cover. They can show you up as everything from a bad speller to a bad guy. You haven't been ashamed until you've shouted at and frightened a child for whom you are the sun. You haven't looked into an honest mirror until you've heard your own stupidity come out of the mouth of your six-year-old boy. Nothing puts the limits of your patience, your ingenuity, your knowledge of American history into larger type than a four-year-old who is both diminished by them and recording them for posterity.

Somehow all the things we do right, all the acts of generosity and juice—the hours of endorsement, the giggles, the sneakers bought and paid for, the jokes understood, the fears calmed, the games played, the cookies baked, the stories read, the plans encouraged—seem like the least we can do, while all the moments of inattention—the thoughtless remark, the symptoms unnoticed, all the small promises broken, even the D-size batteries brought home for a C-size toy—seem like a dereliction of duty, a glimpse into the vastness of our inadequacy.

When I was a boy the Sisters of Mercy convinced me that God was always watching. I know that idea ennobled my behavior; it may even have ennobled my heart. And though, as a man, I'm not persuaded that divine eyes can be bothered with such as me, I do know that his minions, Josh and Rebecca, are watching. And suddenly it matters if I shamble into a room, garble the King's English, drink too much, make a tasteless joke, or act cynical about elections, vulgar about money, or complacent about Mom. Suddenly I'm in a starring role. Suddenly everything about me matters.

OF OTHER HEROES, COURAGEOUS AND TRADEMARKED

Kids have never been especially good at admiring the right people, but this generation has enshrined an all-time trivial cohort. I know, I sound like an old grouchy guy who thinks computers ruined the world, but the facts speak for themselves.

At least we Eisenhower-era kids had the sense to worship Davy Crockett. Here was a self-reliant, strong-limbed, and stout-hearted fellow who could kill a bear for supper and build a cabin by nightfall. But kids today are unimpressed by such feats. When I rented the Disney Davy Crockett movie, starring Fess Parker, and tried to sell the big guy from Tennessee, my gang actually made fun of his hat.

"Oh, right," sneered David from down the block, "a coonskin cap?" This from the boy who won the third-grade essay contest with "My Hero: The Japanese Guy Who Invented Nintendo." This from a kid who admires Alf, the intergalactic television slacker whose idea of handling a situation is to say, "Yo, no problem." Today, kids admire Eric Davis of the Cincinnati Reds—not for all the reasons we admired Willie and The Mick but because he has a no-cut contract. They think Pee Wee Herman's "I know you are, but what am I?" is a suave, all-purpose rejoinder. Call me old-fashioned, but I still like a hero who goes outside every so often.

Parents of America, it's time to rebuild the pantheon of greatness. And where do we start? We start in the toy boxes, those caches full of plastic cartoon totems that have stolen center stage. We've got to shift the paradigm from the Smurfs to higher ground.

In pursuit of brighter visions, stauncher dreams,

here is the debut catalog of a what-if start-up company called Last Best Hope Toys.

The Smart Little Steves

Colorful action figures of little Stevie Jobs and his buddy, Steve Wozniak. Complete with a molded plastic play garage where the boys invent the personal computer industry, this play set includes a handsomely illustrated booklet explaining how the childhood chums set up a humongous trust fund to provide for their parents in their senescence.

Writin' Tommy J

This Founding Father doll, decked out in colorful colonial costume, will recite Jefferson's Declaration of Independence and give a brief speech about the power of the written word. Complete with an authentic eighteenth-century pheasant quill, Writin' Tommy's arms move with a studious author's flourish, and a computer chip actually duplicates the architectural drawings for Monticello.

(Also available in the Founding Father series: John Hancock, equipped with a set of perfectly shaped cursive magnetic letters, and Ben Franklin, complete with kite, key, and instructions for how to combine careers as a scientist and a statesman.)

Chutes 'n Relativity

This delightful board game features a vulcanized rubber model of the frizzy-haired genius, Albert Einstein, and a blackboard inscribed with $e = mc^2$. The whole family will have hours of brainy fun as they join Uncle Albert in a high jinks-packed hunt for the theory that just may unite all the fundamental forces of nature.

The Senator Bill Bradley Jigsaw Puzzle/ Career Planner

This one-thousand-piece, fully laminated, heavy-duty cardboard puzzle assembles into a collage of a cap and gown, a Princeton sweatshirt, a Rhodes Scholar scroll, an NBA championship ring, a three-piece senatorial suit, and a campaign button bearing the quizzical and tantalizing legend, "Bradley for President?"

GI Joe and State Department Josephine

Stored with the traditional camouflage-clad fighting man in a two-chambered—perfectly proper, I assure you—carrying case, the Josephine Auchincloss diplomat doll represents the force of minds, not arms. She comes complete with a seven-point plan for peace in the region, a plan that addresses both the local need for self-determination and United States security requirements.

Barbie in Flats

The classic doll America's girls love with one important modification—her feet are not frozen in a stiletto-heel arch. This nineties twist on the outdated sixties sexist-pig notion of the female form also says, "Hi, I'm Barbie, and I think shoes should be comfortable instead of serving to incline my body so as to encourage some over-wrought male enthusiasm."

OF ROLE MODELS AND ROALD DAHL

The vow to embody probity and surge is, of course, the easy part. The neat trick is figuring out how to be a guide for your kids, how to be influential but not daunting. How do you loom over them but cast no shadow?

The final truth about how to be an example for your kids is in Roald Dahl's novel *Danny, the Champion of the World*. A father teaches his son the grand outlaw art of poaching, and they conspire in a high adventure against the forces of privilege. What we owe the kids is revealed in the boy's description of his father: "It was impossible to be bored in my father's company. He was too sparky a man for that. Plots and plans and new ideas came flying off him like sparks off a grindstone."

Don't steer them. Don't tell them how to think about school, about friends, about tomorrow. Above all, don't pass on mere complaint in the guise of opinion. Al Davis, the buccaneer owner of the Los Angeles Raiders, lives by a slogan coined to get to the simple, vigorous heart of football. "Just win, baby," is the Davis version for nose guards and wide receivers. Just spark, baby, is the Dahl version for moms and dads. Don't tell them anything about politics, about money, about careers. There are many mansions in my father's house. The rules of chivalry are powerful but few. Just spark, baby. The kids will catch fire.

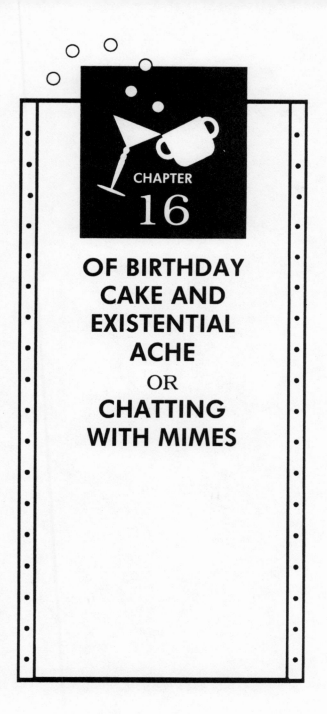

OF BIRTHDAY
CAKE AND
EXISTENTIAL
ACHE
OR
CHATTING
WITH MIMES

As Josh presided over the cheerful clamor of the party marking his seventh birthday, I was struck by the fact that he seemed suddenly fully formed. Until then he'd been a babe, nothing but possibilities. But at that moment, it seemed to me, he bore both the vividness and compromise of history. He was wearing a party cone hat and a luminous smile. I couldn't stop looking at him.

Some of his history showed—the scar on his lip from a Christmas Eve wrestling match with his cousins. But most of it was a secret—the best friend who'd moved away, the teacher who'd scared him silly and made him strong, the stories we'd read that were in there, intact and in pieces. I was stunned by the speediness of time, the wink in which he'd gone from just-hatched to muscled lad. I could feel all his pieces, disappointments, and elations, those memories, happy and not, shaping him into the one of a kind he would become. As the birthday boy held court, offering his chums more cake, I savored the fine improbability of each of us.

But then, as the party began its segue from cake to games, my parental reverie was interrupted by an unholy remembrance of flings past. I had a horrible flashback to previous parties for littler kids. In an instant, as I set up the one-short seating for musical chairs, I recalled a veritable parade of claustrophobic parties—some of which I'd hosted—for three-year-olds, two-year-olds, even one-year-olds. The memories came in rapid-fire rat-a-tat:

- Paper cups tumbling as though in slo-mo through the air
- The juice that used to be in them, floating free, still cup-shaped and headed south
- Gasping for breath while twenty-three children sucked the oxygen from a basement playroom and into their selfish little lungs
- Icing in my eyebrows
- My ears
- My wallet

As Josh lined the kids up for the game, I remembered a party for a two-year-old named Marcy, during which I vowed to hunt down and kill the man who wrote "Happy Birthday to You." In a matter of moments I had swooped from a sentimental colloquy about time and my firstborn to a memory of momentary madness. When Josh's friend Sebastian tugged on my sleeve and suggested I take a rest for a minute, I emerged from my suddenly bleak funk and made myself a promise: to dedicate such energy as I have to putting an end to the toddler birthday bash.

Birthday parties for mere babes may appear, to the casual observer, benign, even joyful. But not so. They are a self-inflicted parental nightmare, the dark side of the preschool years.

Every day across the country parents plan, pay for, and perpetrate parties featuring clowns, mimes, and magicians for kids so small they think rabbits actually live in top hats. Our kids once went to a fourth birthday party with a Roaring Twenties theme—bathtub juice (dozens of Minute Maid boxes in a tub of ice), three mothers dressed as flappers. The parents all got copies of *The Great Gatsby* in their goody bags.

Now, I grant you, we make this kind of fuss for a sweet reason. We're out to make memories, to pack their lives with incident and event. But that's just not the way it works. They don't remember the choo-choo cake complete with caboose and marzipan cowcatcher you spent three days concocting/assembling/deploying. They don't remember the party tape featuring the best of Raffi, Burl Ives, and Bert and Ernie. The fact is, if they remember anything it will be that Jason took their cake.

Compare the list of memories Mom and Dad hope Junior will cherish forever with a list of things the scion actually recalls:

Hope	Reality
The mute Chaplinesque grace of Michel the Mime	A man in white makeup and a blue wig asking where Dad keeps the hooch
The exuberant American high jinks of musical chairs, well played	The music dying and no place to sit
The delicate, indeed, the heartbreaking, fluting of pink cake decoration	Not getting the rose with the delicate, indeed, the heart-breaking fluting

Now if the downside risk here were only a few bad childhood memories, going after a few happy ones might be worth a shot. But the stakes are much higher. The kids, you see, are not the only victims here. For unlike three-year-olds who can't form a thought, parents can't forget. For Mom and Dad, these parties for kids are traumatic events.

In 1986 my sister made a party for her daughter's fourth birthday. Enough to say about the plans that she hand-painted twenty-two napkins with aquatic whale/dolphin Greenpeace ecological scenes. I'll never forget the sound of her voice as I came through the door to pick up my kids: "I said, untie me, Brendan."

But even that isn't the nadir to which party-provoked parents can sink. Consider the story of my friend Hal, who hired a vanilla-white circus pony for his son's third. As dusk settled over the crepe-paper-strewn backyard, I saw him stare down a neighbor boy and say, "One more complaint, Todd, and I shoot Milkshake."

It's a little-known literary fact that when T. S. Eliot (father of three) wrote the famous line, "Between the idea and the reality / Falls the shadow," he was inspired, not by some abstract sense of the gulf between theory and practice, but by an ugly experience he and Mrs. E. had at their youngest's second. The implausible yet inevitable passage from balloon-frocked invitation to the final tantrum in the tree out back can diminish Dad's memory of the early days.

So, in the best interests of parents and consequently children around the word, I ask you to join me in taking The No Birthday Parties for Babies Pledge:

> I shall neither sponsor nor attend a birthday celebration in honor of anybody who is under five years old. Neither shall I offer succor to anyone who does so sponsor or attend. Indeed, I shall dedicate myself to spreading the belief among children that they don't have birthdays until they're five.

Start tonight. Spread the word about The Pledge. Invite Segal from down the block over for coffee and conspiracy. Feel the power of parents united with a purpose. Form cells. Discuss how you can support each other. Start by turning down those perky little invitations. And don't decline politely. Call up and say, "On behalf of the parents of America, I not only decline but denounce the invitation to celebrate Stan, Jr.'s second."

This is no curmudgeon's crusade. Quite the contrary. It's a cause full of hope, hope that we can thrive unburdened by memories of party hats thrown in anger.

In fact, once the kids hit five—OK six—parties are perfectly acceptable. "How but in custom and in ceremony are innocence and beauty born?" wrote Yeats.

How indeed? Remember, however, that once parties are a good idea, it doesn't mean they suddenly get easy. Herewith two vital survival strategies:

PIN THE TAIL ON THE DONKEY: THE MR. O'NEILL VERSION

Nearly every child who has ever played Pin the Tail on the Donkey cheats. They can't help it. Here's the way it goes:

You put the blindfold on them and they adjust it a bit, often so that you can actually see their left eye. "You can't see, can you, Freddy?" you ask disingenuously. "Excuse me, Mr. O'Neill," they say, "I can't even hear you, it's so dark in here." Then you spin them in a circle seven times and watch them proceed to place the paper ass's tail precisely where God put it—at the base of the asinine coccyx. Then they take off the blindfold and act surprised and confident. The only problem is that the next kid will put his tail right on top of Freddy's.

Something has to be done. We have to institute one

short, to-the-point, inviolate, nonnegotiable rule: to wit, only Mr. O'Neill touches the blindfold. If it's too tight, or pulling your hair, or breaking your ears, or scratching your nose, or doing any of the excruciating things that blindfolds apparently do to children, just tell Mr. O'Neill and he'll adjust it for you.

On behalf of the parents of America, all of us put in the position of having to act stupid enough to believe that every kid at the party just happens to have a gyroscopic sense of direction, we have to support this rule. But more important than our own self-respect, we have to act on behalf of the one kid at each party who plays it as it lays, the freckle-faced boy—usually named Jeremy—who, carried away by the cornball challenge of groping toward the donkey in the dark, gamely plants the tail—God bless him—with an honest-as-the-day flourish on your zipper. For Jeremy, we have to strike back, stand up for doing things the right way, instead of the today way.

HOW TO TALK TO A MIME

Chances are that some day you'll find yourself at a kid's party where a grown man paints his face, puts on a body stocking, and pretends that he's (1) climbing a staircase, (2) pulling a rope, or (3) trapped in a glass box and—most vexing of all—that he can't talk. Enduring his performance is bad enough, but harder still is chatting with this guy as he's packing his bag to leave.

Here are your options, the only three things you can possibly say to a mime:

- "I loved your legwork on the rope pull."
- "Your bannister hand on the stair-climb killed me."

- "Words fail me, man." (This last is an old mime in-joke, the ultimate mime compliment, their equivalent of "Socko.")

Any of these remarks will let him know that his work has been appreciated by a member of the cognoscenti, somebody who knows what it's like to spend your days walking into the wind. Now granted, you'll only encourage him. And you may find yourself on a mime mailing list when your kids' birthdays roll around. But remember, for all their high crimes, mimes are people too.

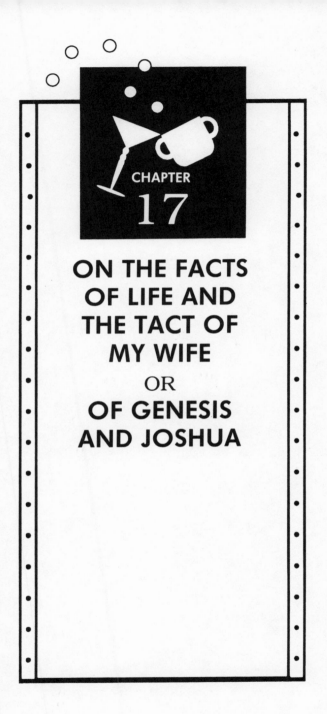

CHAPTER 17

ON THE FACTS OF LIFE AND THE TACT OF MY WIFE

OR

OF GENESIS AND JOSHUA

I was minding my own business, lying on the couch, reading a magazine, when Rebecca came strutting up to me, shoved her stuffed raccoon under her shirt, and said with Shirley Temple spunk, "I'm having a baby, Daddy." I patted her head with what I hoped she'd think was affection, got quietly up, went out, and locked myself in the car.

You see, I'd been through this three years before when her brother started getting curious.

"Babies come from hospitals, Josh," I said in a tone of mild condescension, designed to shame him into silence. I knew where this was headed, to the world of thrust and want, scary to even the mature among us.

"I know that, Daddy," he said, bouncing my condescension back, "but where do they come *from*? How do they get to the hospital?"

"Joshie, you know that," I answered with damnable disingenuousness. "Mommies carry babies in their tummies until it's their birthday."

"I know, Daddy, I know," he continued with forbearance, inhaling as though he would try this once more, "but where do they come *from*?" He knew that I knew what he meant. "Daddy, you're not listening," he said, borrowing a phrase I clearly used too often on him. "How do babies get *into* their mommies' tummies?"

"Oh, oh, oh, I'm sorry, Josh," I said as though I just now figured out what he was after. "Oh, you want to

141

know how babies get *into* their mommies' tummies. Is that what you want to know?"

From over my shoulder I heard Jody laugh.

"Well, that's a horse of a different color," I said in a Munchkin voice, diving on top of him in desperation. "That's a tickle question," I went on, wrestling him to the rug. For twenty-seven marvelous seconds we grappled. He dug his fingers into my ribs, my armpits. Then I said, "I'm tickled out," with a Barrymoresque swoon. "I can't wake up until a certain boy taps me with his magic Ghostbuster gun."

"How, Daddy?" he said.

"How what, son?"

"How do they, Daddy?"

I looked desperately over at Jody. Her expression said two things: first, she wasn't going to rescue me, and second, she'd never seen anything so pathetic in her life.

"Well, they don't exactly get in there, Joshie. They grow in there."

"I know, Daddy, but what makes them grow?"

"Oh, well," I said, suddenly inspired. "That's simple. You mix some mommy juice and some daddy juice with a magic leaf and add a pinch of love."

The sound Jody made is indescribable—part laugh, part gasp, all pity. At that point she decided—"in the best interests of the child," she would say later—to intercede.

"Joshie," she said, "come over here. I've got a book that will explain what Daddy means." They disappeared into his room, leaving me prone on the rug to ponder my performance.

I know. I know. I should have told him. I should have described what used to be called the birds and the bees with joy, right? I owed my son a straightforward explanation of how a baby gets in a mommy's tummy. After all, I spent most of my life explaining things to him.

Lying there in disgrace, I remembered explaining how gasoline made a car go. He had never asked me; I just thought he might be interested.

But, dear reader, lest you judge me harshly, remember this was no young stripling. This was no teenage Huck hearing the siren call. This boy wasn't seven, or six, or even five. This boy was four years, five months, and eleven days old. This boy was a pup, still dusted with pale blond hair. This child still ate off Winnie the Pooh china. Somehow, the art and science of reproduction seemed—oh, I don't know—too serious for him.

I know. I know. Because of what I did Josh will be forever sheepish about sex. I also knew exactly what Jody would say later. She would use joyful, uninhibited words like "dunce" and "good grief."

I foraged for a defense of some kind and settled on an "I'm a victim of my background" strategy. It was, I decided in a flash, all my father's fault. After all, what could you expect from a guy whose father thought the facts of life were that the Democrats would raise taxes and that you had to work all day for your sugar in your tea. I come from a long line of guys who just aren't frank about you know what.

One day, my father, a surgeon and a man of science, was taking a shower. My five-year-old niece Austin, later to achieve fame as Pippi Longstocking, walked in and peeked behind the shower curtain at grandpa. My modest father grabbed the shower curtain and wrapped it demurely around his body.

"Poppy, do you have a penis?" the girl-child asked gaily.

Now it is to his credit that my father was uneasy about his granddaughter getting an eyeful. And it would have been perfectly reasonable had he responded with "Good morning, honey. Poppy would like some privacy." Of course, even better, he might have said, "Of course I do, doll. All men have penises." But no. My father, sire of seven, a man who had spent his life repairing, honoring the human body, a man who could name the blood vessels that enlivened the male member, didn't give either of those answers. No, he looked out, Diana-like, from behind his plastic toga and gave a much shorter, much simpler answer. "Uh . . . uh . . . uh . . . no, no, no, I don't," he said. No, no, and no again, he thrice denied what his granddaughter had clearly just seen. Three times he told her that a penis was not standard male issue.

Lying there on the rug, preparing for Jody's return, I started feeling unexpectedly feisty. With each moment my defensiveness waned. After all, I may be less than enlightened about sex, but compared to the penile Judas whose genes I carried, I was a regular Dr. Ruth. I consoled myself with the idea that even if my baby recipe of juice, leaves, and love had diminished my son's future, at least he and his cousin could be stunted together for the rest of their lives.

I kept building my defense. "Dammit, it *was* daddy juice and mommy juice, I said to the jury in summation. The leaves and the love? Those were just kid details. "Josh knew what I was getting at, Jody," I would later say dismissively. "He's not stupid, you know," I would continue. "And he knows what a metaphor is," I would close, trying to suggest that somebody's mother might be just a tad on the literal side.

The door of Josh's room opened, and Jody came out loaded for bear.

"What's the matter, doll?" I asked, pretending she would surely by now have stopped obsessing about my adorable, inconsequential, morphogenetic fable.

"That," she said, as though I was supposed to know

what she was talking about, "was quite possibly the lamest thing I've ever heard. I mean, really—mommy and daddy juice? A pinch of love? Why didn't you just tell him you found babies in a cabbage patch?"

"That's an old, tired story, Jode," I said, Truman Capote at his most dismissive.

"At least it's clearly a lie," she continued. "Your version is just accurate enough to confuse him completely." I think at that moment she was regretting having mixed her juice with mine.

"Josh knows what I was getting at, Jode," I said.

She said nothing.

"He's not stupid," I continued.

She said nothing.

"He has a way with metaphor," I closed with a bang.

She guffawed. I was grateful for the sound.

I think she was trying to decide which was more preposterous—my account of conception or my defense of it. She shook her head mournfully from side to side, lifted her eyes to mine and said, "He has a way with metaphor?" repeating my phrase as though it were a silly thing to say. Then, for good measure, she repeated it again. "He has a way with metaphor?"

"Yes . . . yes, he does," I said firmly, hopeful that if she was reduced to repeating my lines I had at least blunted her attack.

"Then why," she said, and I could feel a roundhouse right coming, "why is he at this moment crumbling a leaf into a glass of juice and tapping it with a Lincoln Log chimney?"

I said nothing.

She said nothing.

I started to laugh.

So—thank heaven—did she. "You know," she went on, "he prefers your version to the truth."

"Did I ever tell you the story about Austin and my father?"

Later that night I flipped through the frank "joyful" book Jody had offered up to Josh's curiosity. It starred a cartoon sperm cell, wearing a jogging suit, racing toward an eager girly egg with a pink ribbon on her bald, ovoid head. Everybody was smiling. It was, I suppose, truthful. I suppose it did reveal "how" babies were conceived, but it never got past machinery. And it never got near Josh's question, which wasn't a "how?" question but a "where?" question. Worst of all, the book was goofy.

I think there is much to be said for reproduction à la Doc O'Neill. In the world according to my father, babies had nothing to do with eggs, seeds, tubes. In his world, babies were the stuff of he and she, the climax of a taste for each other, the legacy of a collaboration for better or worse. In his mind, babies were made of passion. That's the answer to Josh's question. It may not be accurate, but it is the truth.

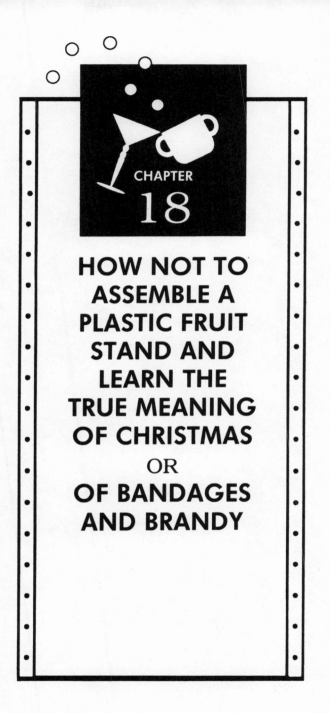

CHAPTER

18

HOW NOT TO ASSEMBLE A PLASTIC FRUIT STAND AND LEARN THE TRUE MEANING OF CHRISTMAS

OR

OF BANDAGES AND BRANDY

Christmas is surely one of the most romantic seasons of family life. Parents and children flutter about in anticipation. Kid dreams of toys unlimited share the air with the redemptive power of love.

And yet beneath the Norman Rockwell fantasy lurks a threat to the serenity of the family hearth. Till now unreported, out of some excessive respect for a sacred time, it has to do with fathers and the task of assembling toys. When the Ghost of Christmas Presents visited me last December, it was not the stuff of holiday viewing.

This is the story of one man's odyssey to Christmas dawn. It is a tale of one-on-one—a molded plastic fruit stand versus yours truly, at five-foot-ten, 168 pounds. It is a tale of two incompetent hands and one by now well-tempered heart. But before the night before, a manly complaint and pathetic excuse.

A DIRECTIONAL PRELUDE

It's well known that only women need to follow directions. All men believe that their instincts will guide them to 495 South or to a well-built playhouse. And though our Daniel Boone gland may make us late for a lot of weddings, it does no damage when it comes to assembling Christmas gifts. For the fact is that toy assembly directions fall into two equally useless categories.

1. Rebus directions. These have no words. Obviously prepared on the cheap by an "international" company, they feature artless drawings of wing nut (j), support strut (k), and plenty of arrows. Unrestrained by language, they invite you to follow—along with dads from Cairo to Quito—the same step-by-step hieroglyphic instructions.

Most often, you've got no shot. To start with, the drawings bear only a passing resemblance to the pieces splayed out in front of you. About the best you can do is put the pieces next to each other and hope. On occasion, physics will burble through and intention will reveal itself. More often, you'll find yourself breaking vital flange (p) off side slat (r) so it matches the one in the drawing.

Though the intricacies of rebus directions will probably remain forever occult, semioticians at Yale have come up with a few educated guesses about the meaning of some of the more common pictographs:

2. Zen Buddhist directions. These equally inscrutable directions are apparently written in an ancient dialect by an Oriental mystic who believes that first

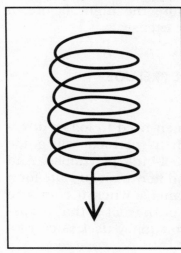

Most experts think this means to twist a part in a counterclockwise direction, then push down hard. However, a vocal minority—including an expert in Mayan cave painting from Trinity College, Dublin—argues that it means to hang the part from a Slinky until it drops to the carpet.

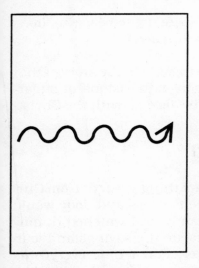

The majority view here is that the wavy line with an arrow suggests a gentle pressure of one part against another. The minority position—in my view persuasive—argues that this is merely a satanic serpent symbol meant to mock anybody who has ever taken Christmas seriously.

there is a mountain, then there is no mountain, then there is. In contrast to rebus directions, these are full of words, just devoid of meaning. Indeed, they aspire to partake of life's infinitude by swallowing their tail. I once spent three hours trying to crack the following koan:

Assemble truck motor (parts c, d, e, f, p & z) before attaching axles (parts l & t) to shimmy sleeves (q), focal posts (v), or anything equally suitable for attaching to.

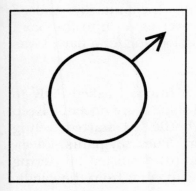

Some feel that this means move a piece forcefully upward and to the right. More likely, however, this international symbol for male means, "Find a real man to help you, sweet stuff."

In no case, however, expect spare tire to be useful. Indeed, be wary of expectation in general.

But enough excuse-making. On to the story of that night, the night that began with visions of sugarplums and became a horrible face-off with the Christmas imp of the perverse.

Christmas Eve began like something straight from Currier & Ives. I would assemble the toys and Jody would wrap gifts as we shared brandy and watched Jimmy Stewart and Donna Reed rescue the savings and loan from the churlish Mr. Potter. For a time everything went smoothly. I slapped together a Ghostbusters Lab with fatherly flair, set up an electric train. Jody was sticking candy canes on everything.

But when I got to the fruit stand—forty-three pieces, trademarked, all rights reserved—I recognized the first signs of toy-assembly terror:

- I tried to force the tiny little fruit bin into the fruit-bin display slot. At first, I pushed gently, but soon with enough force to bow out the little yellow sides of the bin.
- Then I started peeking involuntarily—indeed compulsively—over and over again into the box I knew was empty. I wasn't looking for a part; I was looking for help.

Then things went south in a hurry. I asked Jody to bring me a tub of butter and some more hooch. ("Keep the glass, babe, bring the bottle.") I started feeling clammy and took off my shirt. Then my pants. I accidentally swallowed dowel cap (d). I started muttering about missing pieces and cheap labor from the Pacific

Rim. Dear reader, within fifteen minutes, the man who had flirted with fantasies of carving a rocking horse from the fallen oak out back was on his hands and knees in his underwear, whacking a plastic cash register with the noggin of a Cabbage Patch Kid.

It got worse. When Jody pointed out, at 1 A.M., that the fruit stand was leaning to the left, I replied that if the kids didn't like it they could lump it. When she suggested that we turn in and put all this stuff together in the morning, I told her I already had a mother. She kissed my sweaty crown, said, "Merry Christmas, Daddy," and went to settle down for a long winter's nap.

Over the next seven hours, my desperation was enhanced by my aloneness. I struggled with the fruit stand, a table soccer game, a snazzy yellow bike, and a road racing set that required a soldering gun. By 2 A.M. I had directions between my teeth. By 3 a corkscrew was in there with them. All told that night, I used three wrenches, two pairs of pliers (one needlenose), both kinds of screwdrivers, sandpaper, the poker from the fireplace, the blade of a hacksaw, some olive oil, and a fork. At exactly 5:14—according to the records from the emergency room—I had used my T-shirt as a tourniquet. Norman Rockwell had given way to Norman Bates.

By the early rays of morning I was not the husband and father who had poured out a cheerful cascade of fruit-stand parts. Like the mild-mannered citizen who, trapped in the wilderness, reverts to an elemental state, I was a man transformed, stripped of social niceties like grammar and clothing. I felt wild and anonymous. I had become a Christmas savage.

When the kids came bursting downstairs, they didn't notice me lurking behind the chair in the corner. I watched them through the clear, desperate coyote eyes of my humiliation. As they bounced among the no-denying-it beautifully assembled treasures, I felt simple and mute; I felt their pleasure in my bones. My affection for them seemed fierce.

I could have paid to have all those toys assembled. No question, my ambition in doing it myself was prideful. I longed to pass my feeling for the kids through my hands. And in my comeuppance for that small sin, I got a lesson in the modest heart of Christmas and children.

Consider: The Nativity is the birthday of a guy who, when asked who he was didn't refer to his history, his accomplishments, his skills, his way with a plastic fruit stand, but said, "I am." Not exactly a hard sell. No résumé-enhancer, he. His love was like drawing breath. And so is the children's love uncredentialed. It comes clean and plain, unaccomplished and strong.

After two hours of Yuletide glee, I staggered upstairs and crawled into my Christmas bed. As I drifted—unshaven, incompetent, and undone—into half-sleep, I felt defenseless and at home. I could feel the wind on my face.

God bless us, everyone.

TWO YULE RULES

Fathers of the world, if you have any pride at all: *Never claim you did a lousy job because all the pieces weren't in the box.* This only makes you look like a klutz who is also a bad sport. There are few things less cool than a fully grown man contending that what might have been a little log cabin looks like something from Brancusi's depressed period because some piece-worker from Sri Lanka left out a washer. Besides, the fact is that somehow—God knows how—all the pieces are always in the box. If axle girdle (m) appears to be missing, it's because you mistook it for hub cover (y).

So, *never throw out leftover pieces.* By Valentine's Day that S-shaped piece will be revealed to you as brace bridle (f), and you'll be able to make the log cabin stand at attention.

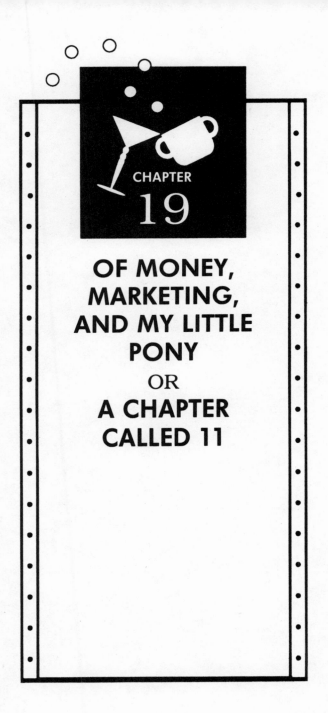

CHAPTER

19

OF MONEY, MARKETING, AND MY LITTLE PONY

OR

A CHAPTER CALLED 11

Like the hero of Dante's *Inferno* I found myself at midlife in a dark wood. His was the underworld; mine was Chapter 11, bankruptcy. I was brought to the brink of penury not by gambling or drink, not by reckless enterprise nor spiritual unease. No, I was seduced by a far more insidious siren—the va-va-va-voom toy totem who's been stringing Ken along for years.

I was undone by Barbie.

My troubles began with a modest purchase—one 12-inch tall plastic Barbie doll for Rebecca. But my descent was headlong. I bought Barbie's sister, Skipper; then her three identical friends Belinda, Mikko, and Nikki. Then came the playsets—the Barbie Music Awards, Doctor Barbie, Barbie's Sunshine Holiday. Then I whirled into a fashion phase. I bought everything from a Barbie bikini to an itsy-bitsy strapless number for the Oscars. Then I tore through the accessories—from the makeup kits to the Barbie omelet pan. I finally bottomed out when I spent $14.95 for Barbie's pet cockatoo, Tahiti.

Oh, Barbie was my nemesis, but my problem went deeper than the blond bombshell. Mine is an ugly and singularly American story of toy excess. Over the last three years I've spent close to $2 million in the building genus alone (Duplos, Construx, Tinkertoys, et al.,), another mil on magic kits, and just a tad south of $400,000 on teensy-weensy dinette sets. Had I passed on the Teenage Mutant Ninja Turtles, the kids might have learned organic chemistry in the state-of-the-art

O'Neill Labs at Princeton. Now I can only hope college isn't in their plans.

I'm still not sure why I frittered away what the people at Citibank might one day have referred to as The O'Neill Trust on plastic action figures, video games, and "Go to the Head of the Class." I guess I did it just so I wouldn't have to explain to the kids they couldn't have the Airborne Ooze Assault Weapon. I have racked my brain for some self-aggrandizing explanation. Finally, one day, just short of Josh's fifth birthday, on yet another trip to the toy supermarket, it came to me.

I wasn't just a weak fool who had abandoned his fiduciary responsibility to his family. I was no gutless yes man, controlled by his indiscriminately acquisitive children. No, I had a good reason for bringing us to the edge of financial ruin.

As the door open-sesamed in front of us, Josh surged away into the paradise of toys. He was ready to roll, optimistic about the next hour. Without warning he bolted down the aisle.

"Oh, Daddy," he gasped, sneakers squeaking him to a stop. "Oh, Daddy, can we buy this? Please, Daddy, please. I saw this guy on TV. He's great. He talks. Really, Dad, he can talk. Not like Becky's doll, Daddy. He really talks." This last "talks" was in verbal italics. Josh wanted me to understand that this stuffed something-or-other—it appeared to be half bear, half dachshund, mostly sunglasses—talked, not like Becky's beloved if repetitive Miss Susan, but more, I gather, in the manner of Mario Cuomo.

"He really talks, Daddy," he said, catching my peek at the price tag. "Becky would like him too," he continued, pulling out all the stops.

Here was a parent's quandary. Only a prodigal father

would spend the better part of a hundred dollars on something the boy would give to the mailman by Friday. But I didn't bring my son to this palace of trade-marked dreams just to point out a few of the items he couldn't have.

"I don't think that's a good toy, pally. Let's look around," I said hopefully. "I bet you'll find something you like more."

"How many dollars does he cost, Daddy?" Josh asked, suspicious that cost had something to do with my opinion.

"A hundred dollars, Josh."

"Is that a lot?"

"Yes, son, that's a lot."

"Don't we have a hundred dollars, Daddy?" he said with what I hoped was surprise but I feared was condescension.

"Yes, we have a hundred dollars," I whispered, assuming he was talking about total family assets, real estate included.

I looked around defensively. A woman by the pogo sticks turned away. "But that's not the point, Josh," I said. "The point is the price is unreasonable." I doubted that I ever asked my father how much money he had. I also doubted, however, that my father ever made me listen to words like *unreasonable.* He'd have either popped for the hundred without a lot of palaver or refused to explain why we were taking a skip on the talking mutt.

We continued our cruise through toy heaven, gabbing about the pros and cons of mechanical lizards and baby chemistry sets. Josh twice mentioned our hundred-dollar talking friend, as though going on record that this remained an open question. Of course, when I pictured setting fire to a C-note, the question seemed less open to me than it probably did to him. But no matter. Deliverance was at hand.

Josh surged suddenly away, a boy on a mission. As he ran, his voice drifted back over his head. "Oh, Daddy, Daddy," he said, "can we get this? This is the funnest thing. I hope I can get it, Daddy." He was already out of breath and steaming down the aisle toward a big display. I squinted into the distance as he grabbed something and started back.

"Oh, Daddy, Daddy," he said, handing me his treasure. "I'm sure this is reasonable," he said, I think without sarcasm. "It really is the funnest."

It was a big plastic weapon of some kind. It wasn't a gun, Daddy, he explained, it was a "projector." It didn't shoot bullets, but "just only light, Daddy." Near as I could tell from his description, it flashed pictures of bad guys on the wall so you and your friends could stand around and jeer at them.

"Is it, Daddy?"

"Is it what, Joshie?"

"Reasonable, Daddy, is it reasonable?" he said, a little bit annoyed with me.

"Yes, this is reasonable," I lied, grateful to have just saved eighty bucks. "This looks great. Let's bring this home. Mommy loves things that aren't guns."

He grabbed it from me, hugged it, and then kissed its barrel. I wondered if a child could be too enthusiastic about something made of plastic.

On the way home, Josh sat in the back of the car exploring, flipping switches, uncovering the assets of his sidearm. As I drove I actually figured out why parents buy toys for kids in spite of our better judgment.

The first reason is simple: The kids want it. The second is a little more complex. We like to think that happy children come from many careful and affectionate days. But the suspicion lingers that caprice is at large as well. The suspicion lingers that their eventual deal with the world has only a little to do with care and feeding, but that there is a switch, a who-knows-when and once-in-a-lifetime moment of opportunity, in which their enthusiasm—for baseball or art or their sister—is fired.

The legend of Einstein maintains that a diffident, disconnected four-year-old mind took wing—to eventually remake our understanding of time and matter—when Uncle Hans gave him a compass for his birthday. According to Louis L'Amour, a quick glimpse of a gunfighter stamped his three-year-old brain, leading to both a passion for the Old West and zillions in royalties. The suspicion lingers that our kids' talents—for music or happiness—may have no more to do with the quality of our stewardship than they do with some accident, a goofy afternoon of zapping bad guys with an overpriced plastic object of a particular weight and texture. The suspicion lingers that a gun that shoots just only light, Daddy, may make a difference.

That night on my lockup rounds I found Josh cuddled up with his new toy in the crook of his arm. When I kissed him he stirred. "Where's my gun, Daddy?" he said, fuzzy with sleep.

"Where's your *what*, Josh?" I said, teasing the drowsy boy.

"I mean my projector, Dad," he said, smiling through sleep, up for the game, even at 1 A.M. From the start he has never forgotten anything between us.

"Right here, it's right here, son," I said, moving it over on his pillow.

I imagined the toy's future—twenty-four hours from now, forgotten under the couch, twenty-four years from now, recollected, I hoped, with a ruddy memory of me. I imagined little doors opening for little pilgrim souls.

As Josh went back to sleep, a peach-pink cameo in

the half-light, I was struck by the fact that nothing just like him had ever happened before or would ever happen again.

Though psychologically it helped me to know I was not just another out-of-control addict but just guilty of longing to make my kids possible, financially, that wisdom helped me not at all. I continued to spend for another three months, until one day, using a pair of Cookie Monster scissors, an adolescent cashier at Uncle Lonnie's Toy Universe cut my credit card in half. Once that happened there was nowhere to hide. The disdain of a sophomore in a fez is tough to finesse.

But slowly, my loyal wife beside me, I got better. I came out of my toy swoon intact—impoverished, to be sure, but intact. I even learned a few hard-won lessons. For example:

- That the IRS has never in its history allowed a Slinky as a business deduction
- That Silly Putty has next to no resale value
- That when it comes to collateral, loan officers are generally underwhelmed by the Nintendo Power Glove

But most important, I learned that selling toys is the ultimate capitalist venture. Getting a budget-minded mom to waste $12.95 on a bucket of neon ecto-goop demands a sinister mercantile wit. I learned marketing skills which will, with a little luck, lead me back to solvency. If nothing else, I've learned from the toy companies, who sucked the marrow from my financial bones, how to spin off a new product from an old reliable. And you can be sure that whatever O'Neill-

Friedman Enterprises turns out to sell, we'll be out in front of the curve on the art of line extension.

Even the companies most often lionized for their marketing moxie could take a page from the honchos at Hasbro, Ideal, and Fisher-Price and consider these new product launches.

The Honda Accord's Best Friend, Randi

This car would be in every way identical to the hugely successful Accord, except that it would come with a friendship diary in the glove box.

Mrs. Reebok

Like Mrs. Potatohead, this new athletic shoe would be distinguished from her husband only by a pair of earrings and a cunning pink clutch. (The same extended family strategy could lead to Mrs. Coffee, Mrs. Clean, and Mr. Paul's Fishsticks.)

The Pepsi Babies

In the retrogenetic line extension tradition of The Muppet Babies and the Flintstone Kids, this new soft drink would be the old classic when just a sprout, packaged in a slightly smaller bottle and complete with a teensy baby rattle.

The Apple II, Wildlife Model

In the tradition of the Barbie endangered species series, which sells Barbie hugging a baby seal (or wolf or you-name-the-not-too-many-left creature), this home computer would have not only all the power and versatility of the unadorned Apple II but a small magnetic panda to perch over the VDT in charming reminder that we've got to protect the habitats of the other passengers on Starship Earth.

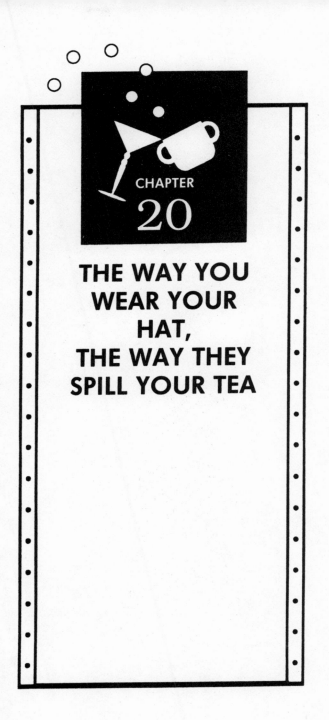

CHAPTER

20

THE WAY YOU
WEAR YOUR
HAT,
THE WAY THEY
SPILL YOUR TEA

In the Disney cartoon classic of dog love, Lady's roguish inamorato, Tramp, summarizes one of the premier parental obligations. He leads the refined society spaniel to the crest of a hill overlooking his mongrel domain and invites her to its unwashed adventures. When she demurs, intimidated by the rough-and-ready of real life, the canine Kerouac exhorts her to reconsider. "Life on a leash," he says, "is no life at all. You better get started on some memories."

Mom and Dad are in charge of the memories.

My parents were masters. They showcased the world with an enthusiasm equal to the word's origin. ("Charged with God," my father told me as he commended me off to college and my life.) Egged on by Mom and Dad's appreciation, the discrete pleasures of the commonplace—from a glass of chocolate milk to a just-raked pile of leaves—came out of hiding for their children.

From the start I had hoped to do the same, give my kids juicy memories. We would go on expeditions to exotic strands. But, more important, we would make a gift of every plain old day. When Josh and Rebecca came to term, they would be vivid, embedded by and in the textures, scents, and sense of our adventure. But in my eagerness to equip the kids with memories, to give them an anthology of impressions equal to the one my parents had given all of us, I became a fool. Like the tragic heroes of legend, I overreached and I achieved only the pale parody of all those who mimic the masters.

Jody says the word *hero* is inappropriate in any context concerning my forays as Father Memory. In support of her view she submitted a secret tape recording including the following exchanges. (The parenthetical text was added by my wife on making the transcripts):

DAD: (*at the wheel rounding a curve in a country road and pointing to what might be an equine speck in a distant pasture*) Hey, look at the horses, kids.

REBECCA: (*trying to stretch up from her seat belt and see out the window*) Where, Daddy?

DAD: (*apparently determined that "horses in a meadow" will enter the memory bank*) Right there, doll, you see those spots underneath the big puffy cloud? Those are horses.

REBECCA: (*as the car swoops around a curve into the next vista, an unbearable sense of loss in her voice*) I can't see, Daddy. Where?

The transcript had the following marginal notation in Jody's hand: "Daughter cried halfway to Goshen."

I meant well. That memory—the supple grace of horses at lazy gallop—was to be a gift from Mom and Dad. Didn't happen. Instead, three months after that trip up the Hudson Valley, my daughter woke up frantic at 3 A.M., muttering, "Where are the horses, Daddy? I can't see the horses." Rebecca had a memory, all right—of something wonderful just beyond her reach.

After hearing the tape I vowed to make it up to her. I would see to it that she didn't miss the horses. But I had misunderstood the problem and things only got worse. If Jody's tapes can be believed, this conversation took place just three weeks later:

DAD: Hey kids, look at the waterfall.

REBECCA: (*once again from the backseat*) Mommy, do I have to?

JODY: No, babe, you can keep coloring. Daddy's just excited to be with us.

After playing me this recording, punching the buttons on her machine with prosecutorial glee, Jody took the Shakespeare from the shelf and started reading to me "Speak the speech I pray you," she began, in what I gather was her idea of an Elizabethan accent, "as I pronounced it to you, trippingly on the tongue . . . Do not saw the air too much with your hand." Apparently she felt I should consider Hamlet's caution to his players. She went on to warn me against tearing "a passion to tatters" and concluded with a hauteur most charitably described as unattractive. "Hamlet, Act III, Scene 2," she said, thwumping the huge book closed.

But unfortunately her high-handedness couldn't obscure the wisdom of her point. My failing wasn't being too slow, pointing things out just as they vanished from view, my crime was doing play-by-play on our life, treading on the heels of our experience. What my folks did without adjectives, I did with promotional copy on behalf of the world. I was trying to help the kids remember stuff before it happened to them.

Still, seeing the problem was one thing; solving it quite another.

The worst was yet to come.

The day began with a summer vacation breakfast for four in a restaurant on the shore—coffee, o.j., blueberry pancakes, kids glowing, madly saying please and thank you. Jody looked tanned and happy, as though this was precisely what she had imagined. As I cut the kids' flapjacks, I worried that the pleasures of this morning meal were too subtle for Josh and Rebecca. To them this may have appeared to be just breakfast, instead of a sacrament. The thought that they would forget this session of syrup and sun ruined my enjoyment of it.

But Providence interceded. On the way out I noticed for sale by the cashier a checker set for the ages. A rock-solid wooden board and—here's the kicker—instead of mere conventional disklike checkers, twenty-four chubby little wooden apples—dozen red, dozen green. This had memory written all over it. I imagined each of the following things:

- This durable checker set being a companion through the years
- Yours truly at fifty-seven, taking it manfully down from a shelf in the library to play with Rebecca's kids
- The kids—undone by grief over my death—taking the checkers to probate

This checker set was a "hook." It could fix this breakfast and this summer in the kids' ancestral memory. And so, I paid thirty bucks for this time machine.

That night, the first time we played, I heard myself giving Josh a stuffy little lecture about how lucky we were to have such a nice checker set. Four minutes later, I told him not to tap the captured apples together while he planned his attack on the rest of my fruit. I became obsessed with the object that was supposed to stand for our breakfast and that summer.

Once, when Rebecca picked up an apple and playfully pretended to take a bite out of it, I said, "Rebecca, these are not toys." She simply turned and retreated, filing away a memory, all right—not of family feeling, but of her ferretlike father counting little wooden apples and locking them in the safe. Josh just looked at me and said, "Yes they are, Dad. Checkers are too toys."

Finally, after about three weeks of checkers à la Queeg, two of the green apples disappeared. Under interrogation, Jody said she had seen the dog chomping on something colorful and loud. To me it sounded more like a confession than mere testimony. At the time I wondered whether the marriage was going to work out. But that night, I came to my senses when Jody played me a recording of a checker game with Josh, what I now think of as "the penultimate tape." Allow me if you will, dear reader, to just admit that it included each of the following sound bites:

- "Someday you'll probably tell your son about that quadruple jump, don't you think, Josh?"
- "Just in case anything should happen to the checkers, son, here's the number of the home owner's policy."

It also had two garbled phrases that Jody claimed were, "heirloom" and "from generation unto generation."

Jody later admitted—no, boasted—that she had taken the two apples to save her children from a father who had lost his way.

It was a cruel shock, but it worked.

I'm cured.

Really, I am.

Really.

I've learned to trust the world to get attention and the kids to notice a thing or two.

Still, parenthood is a maelstrom of recall, a litany of objects, tastes, and sounds that both summon the far-away past and accrete into the legends of the future. Parenthood is eating your first Mallomar in sixteen years and the instant memory of magic Mom moments after school. Parenthood is the scent of a wood-burning set at full singe and the conjuring of your brother Kevin at eleven, madness in his eye, volunteering to carve sister Kathy's initials in her bed frame. Parenthood brings your own parents into your life—with luck as a sweet, grandparently presence, without as ghosts at the banquet. Everything from the dainty but sure adhesion of Colorforms to the sound of the phrase "I'm telling," from the bouquet of a box of crayons to the cadence of classic kids' books rings a distant bell, floats you back through your own history. Parenthood is, in the words of Yogi Berra, Dale's dad, "déjà vu, all over again."

And so, weakened by the touching legend of themselves when young, Mom and Dad become slaves to sentiment. For something to be significant it need only have happened to us.

Every February, in honor of our wedding anniversary, Jody and I go out to a dinner for two—a meal at which nobody orders a cheesedog or Hawaiian punch, nobody throws anything, and nobody has to apologize to nearby diners. And though our ambition is a journey back to the Romeo and Juliet time before we were so burdened, we inevitably end up trading exultations about the kids. We pass back and forth unwinnowed husks of memories, mere word cues, which are, through some sweet alchemy, as eloquent as the evening wind.

"Storyland," she'll toss across the table.

"Vanilla," I'll respond without rhyme or reason, but just right.

"*The Lion, the Witch and the Wardrobe*," she'll confess over dessert.

"Stomach singing," I'll offer over cognac.

We burnish the past to a high sheen. All the places we've been, the tantrums we've endured, the out-of-nowhere jokes, the amusements, anxiety, the happy and dark events are shaped into a story, not just of what happened but of what we've hoped.

Though I'm still a madman for memories, I do manage to keep it most often to myself. In fact, it's not uncommon these days for Josh or Rebecca to point out the mundane wonder of something or other to me.

And now, years after the apple checker set has crumbled into the entropic hug of our home, every so often one of the apples will tumble out of a barrel of Tinkertoys, making it in an instant clear that a small lonely shard is a far richer link to that summer than the pristine pack of *pommes de checkers* could ever have been. After all, memories always come in pieces. In the words of Woody Allen, it's tough to tell whether they're something we have or something we've lost.

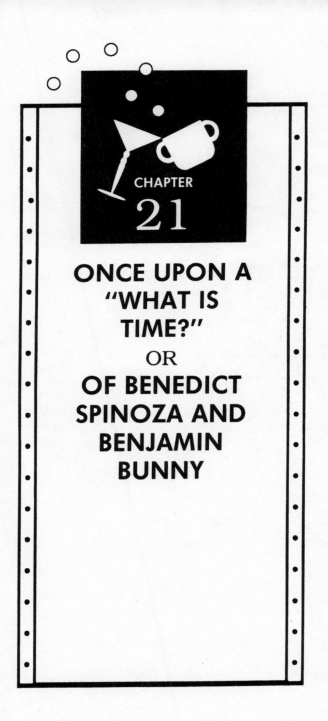

CHAPTER

21

ONCE UPON A
"WHAT IS
TIME?"
OR
OF BENEDICT
SPINOZA AND
BENJAMIN
BUNNY

Kids' books should come with a warning label. They can be dangerous—not to your physical well-being but to your peace of mind. Indeed, prolonged exposure to children's literature can make you question everything in which you once fervently believed, change you from a down-to-earth home owner to a fanciful fool, from solid citizen to mushy romantic.

At first glance, the kid classics appear to be benign, cheerful tools of the establishment—a bushy-tailed Talmud of virtues from compassion to pluck. But Beatrix Potter and her cohort aren't straight-ahead and civic at all. They are, quite the opposite, a quilted cadre of subversion. Indeed, parents who spend a lot of time in the good-natured worlds of Stuart Little, Madeline, Curious George, and Dr. Seuss will inevitably end up wrestling with those epistemological *Ur*-questions that made Spinoza such a bore at dinner parties. To wit: What is real? and What is not?

It all begins innocently enough. Indeed, the first sign that you're headed to a crisis of faith is nothing more sinister than an unexpected lilt in your language. You start using words like *frolic* and *bamboozle* and *zoom*. You start calling your friends *chums*. You describe a piece of pie as *scrumdiddlyicious;* your favorite aunt as *splendid*. You are never merely confused, but *befuddled, bewildered, vexed,* or *puzzled*. Or perhaps you'll be *at sixes and sevens*. Every nag is Black Beauty;

every crowd, a *merry band*. Regular old grown-up talk is supplanted by a cheerful diction of kid lit that is part magic and part can-do.

Then, after the bouncy words come the absurdly sunny thoughts. If you read about enough characters like William Steig's hound hero, Dominic, who is "filled with adoration of the visible world," you start to think anything's possible. And therein lies the seditious threat to your niche in this particular nuts-and-bolts world. The effusiveness of kids' books gets you into some deep philosophical water. For if even gravity is no law, but just an option, then reality is amenable to will and imagining.

Mom and Dad, who have spent most of a lifetime getting used to the dreary, but thank-you-very-much reliable, rational bedrock of Western civilization, are suddenly immersed in a world where magic matters more than manners. The journey is full of dangers, especially in that most grown-up of spheres, the work world. Pollyanna isn't welcome among the privateers.

Consider the cases of three parent/employees who couldn't control the upside urge engendered by kid lit.

- The mother who suggested dealing with market-share erosion through the "Tinkerbell strategy," which encouraged everybody at the sales conference to clap if they believed they could reclaim lost shelf space
- The lawyer, father of three, whose innocent client got fifteen to life because Dad cited Thidwick the Big-Hearted Moose instead of Learned Hand
- The night-shift supervisor who sought productivity enhancements by requiring all line personnel to read *The Little Engine that Could*

Still, the professional pitfalls of kids' literature are outweighed by the spiritual benefits. Under its sway, I have ascended—by increments and without my consent—past fact to spirit, to the idea that much of what used to seem so urgent, earnest things like careers, headlines, money in the bank, are so much camouflage for a world informed by a deep magic. In kids' books, there is always a deeper magic, a redoubt for our dreams.

Beyond that, the stories will give you and the kids a common language. After all, much of the stuff on your mind—that registered letter from the bank, the fact that the Sixers are one loss from elimination—is Greek to the next generation. And God knows, the exhilarations and fears of boys and girls can be occult to a jaded grown-up heart. But the boisterous adventures of Amelia Bedelia and Encyclopedia Brown are a lingua franca in which you can yammer all day.

For the entire summer of 1989, Josh and I talked about little else but the adventures of Peter and Susan and Edmund and Lucy in the land of Narnia. Like any shared parlance of allusion, the C. S. Lewis stories linked us. They were a culture at which we were equally fluent. Often trading speculations about the fate of the great generous lion, Aslan, we heard each other far more clearly than ordinary life would allow.

THE COME-HITHER OF *CHARLOTTE'S WEB*

When most people think about romantic novels, noisy tales of war and passion—stories like *Gone with the Wind* and *Doctor Zhivago*—come to mind. But these are merely clamorous stories. The most romantic novel of all time doesn't have a single battle or breathless embrace. And its only quivering loins are of pork.

The week that Josh and Becky and I spent reading

E. B. White's *Charlotte's Web* was one of the sweetest interludes of my life. It's required reading for all kids and parents who care about either friendship or Planet Earth.

Wilbur the pig's overtures of friendship are spurned by the barnyard gang—the goose, the lamb, even Templeton, the sarcastic lowest-of-low rat. But when a cheerful spider, Charlotte, calls "Salutations" from her web in the barn doorway, it's the start of a beautiful relationship.

Charlotte concocts a plan to save Wilbur from the holiday fate that awaits all spring pigs. She spells out the message "Some pig" in her web over Wilbur's pen. Needless to say, when farmer Zuckerman sees the message, Wilbur's destiny shifts from Christmas ham to celebrity hog.

Charlotte assures Wilbur's future by spelling out new web messages. Eventually, although she isn't feeling well, Charlotte goes to the county fair to show Wilbur off. As she languishes and dies, her last wish is that Wilbur take her egg sac, her masterpiece of web spinning, back to the Zuckermans' barn.

Wilbur does and watches over the egg sac until Charlotte's kids are born. "I am a friend of your mother's," he says to them on their emergence. The story concludes:

> Wilbur never forgot Charlotte. Although he loved her children and grandchildren dearly, none of the new spiders ever quite took her place in his heart. She was in a class by herself. It is not often that someone comes along who is a true friend and a good writer. Charlotte was both.

By the time I read the last word—one child snuggled into each arm on our bed—I felt, through my sadness, unsullied, brand-new, as innocent as the lamb. And I felt hopeful that this sweet legend of nature and nurture, this encomium to the earth would linger in the kids' minds, endowing them through their days with the art of small seasonal pleasures and the gift of unadorned affection.

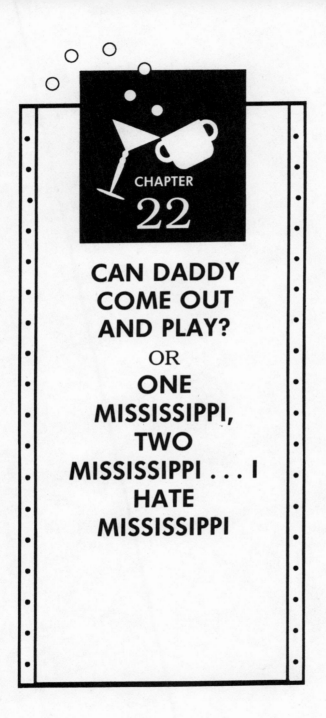

CHAPTER

22

**CAN DADDY
COME OUT
AND PLAY?**

OR

**ONE
MISSISSIPPI,
TWO
MISSISSIPPI . . . I
HATE
MISSISSIPPI**

But, Daddy, you can be the chicken."

Apparently this was supposed to make me change my mind. But in fact it only stiffened my resolve. My polite demurral to Josh's invitation to join him and his cousins in the "magic egg game" would stand. You see, I had been the big boss chicken before.

"No thanks, son," I said with what sounded like sarcasm but was only a necessary steadfastness in my early morning stupor, "I'm just going to sit here and read the paper." And sit there I did—plunked into an Adirondack chair, sucking on a cup of coffee, and lazing through news of mergers, murders, and ninth-inning magic. It had been a long journey to that chair.

I'm allergic to kids' games. In the rest of the package of parenthood I'm a solid B, but when it comes to kids' games—from Hide and Go Seek, Freeze Tag, the "magic egg game," and board games like Clue and Mouse Trap by Ideal to those games of pretend where these plastic guys are trying to escape from those other plastic guys before the enchanted cave is flooded—I'm helpless.

I can spend endless hours talking to children, wrestling with them, even just looking at them. And when it comes to anything that can properly be called a sport, I'm your guy. If you're six and need a batting-practice pitcher, I'll serve 'em up till dark. But you thwap down a colorful laminated board in front of me and I feel a burning sensation in my throat.

Some parents look at a game spinner and see:

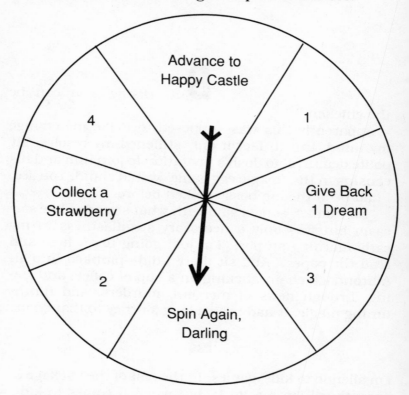

Not me. I look at the same device and feel short of breath (see following page).

To me, Chutes and Ladders is a choke hold; Parcheesi a cave-in at Tunnel Nine.

For the time I tried to characterize my problem as a virtue. I'm just one of those American guys, so went the riff, without a gene for leisure. But Jody averred that in that case I probably wouldn't have invested three and half hours gaping at a football game where the loser got top draft pick. Though certain people don't understand that one blue-chip running back can renovate a whole franchise, as usual Mom had made her point. My dread

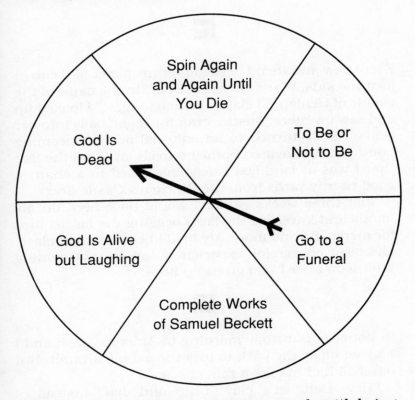

of Red Light-Green Light had nothing to do with being hardworking.

Then I tried to hide behind a "theory" of parenting. Daddy, I argued, wasn't supposed to be "It." Chuckie could be it. Or Shlomo. Or Maggie. Or Duke. But not Dad. If you made Dad "It," you upset an authority-figure construct that kids need if they're to grow up with respect for anything at all. Even I didn't buy this one.

Then I tried snide. Sure, the kids could live in the moment; they didn't have to live at the office. Sure, they had time to be undiminished, at play in the fields of the Lord. Not me; I had chores to do.

None of these stances helped either me or the children.

Every now and then I peeked over my paper and cup of jo at the kids. When I heard a cry of "In the name of the people of Henland, I claim the magic eggs," I looked up and saw my niece, Austin, cramming golf balls into her jeans. As I returned to an editorial on an upcoming bond issue, I savored both the fresh java and the fact that I was at long last safely ensconced in a chair, a good twenty yards from the Chicken's Castle Coop.

Just three weeks earlier I would have been on my hands and knees on the lawn begging the fascist bird for mercy. But no more. My final liberation took place, like most conversion experiences, on an unassuming afternoon after I had given up hope.

In honor of Saturday morning in America, Josh and I had set off to the park to toss the old pill around. But baseball had to take a rain check.

"Hey, Dad, let's play "Chip and Jeff" instead of catch," Josh said blithely as though it were a much better game.

"OK, pal," I said, despondent but determined to follow his lead, "how do you play?"

"We have to find the magic crystals without getting burned by the lava."

My heart stopped. Hot lava had nothing to do with the hot corner. The phrase "magic crystals" wasn't good news.

Chip (in this case, me) and Jeff (apparently always Josh) are adventurers whose assignment is to figure out the codes, locate the crystals, assemble them into the pyramid of power, and banish the evil slave master, Wizgar. They have to do all this while hopping from the monkey bars to the park benches or the low wall or anything slightly elevated that would keep them from standing on the hot lava, more commonly known as the ground, for longer than a count of ten. Unless you had the lava boots—which could only be attained by some impossibly heroic act—ten seconds on the lava and you were, according to Josh, "dead meat."

This game had invisible guards and power chips that could easily have been mistaken for pieces of tree bark. It featured incantations as well as lava wands and lava capsules, which you either wanted because they made you invincible or dreaded because they made you ash.

I followed orders, a faithful Chip. I snuck (for parents this is a word, past tense of *sneak*) around the sandbox and looked for the code. I crawled down the slide, hopped across the lava, and pushed the tire swing to see if Wizgar had been in this level of the kingdom. I was the ultimate grunt. I did as I was told.

Every now and then, Josh—I mean, Jeff—would ask my advice. "We've got to get past the guard, Chip," he'd say, pointing to an eighteen-month-old playing with a sand-sifter. "What should we do?"

"Use a lava capsule?" I tried. He looked at me as though maybe I was one of Wizgar's men in disguise.

Every now and then I would look longingly over at the fathers and sons tossing the old pill around and suggest that we might take a break.

"Hey, Josh, you wanna toss the old pill around a bit?"

"Chip, you can't play baseball on lava," he said, apparently wondering if I was even up to the none-too-demanding sidekick role.

And so it went. On and on and on and on. Buffeted by Jeff's directives I bounced from swing set to seesaw, a fully grown man flattening himself against magic trees in a ruleless nightmare of fantasy, a capricious chaos of counting and skipping.

I remember the following exchange:

JEFF: (*whooshing down a slide*):   Chip, we've got to find the prince before he meets the final monster. You know what to do. (This last was not a question; it was an assumption.)

CHIP: Use a lava capsule?

JEFF: No, summon the whirlwind.

JEFF: Quick, now's the time, Chip.

CHIP: The lava capsule?

JEFF: No, use the wand of Gormlech from the fountain of time.

Once I got assertive and tried a strategic suggestion of my own.

CHIP: Maybe the crystals are buried and we should summon the magic dwarves to help us find them?

JEFF: What are you talking about, Chip? There are no magic dwarves.

CHIP: Yes, there are, Jeff, they live in the seventh circle and can be called to earth with this baseball-like sphere.

Jeff's expression said, "Get a grip, Chip."

My humiliation was complete when Jeff, the general who had prudently held his fire, suddenly shouted, "Now, Chip, strike now . . . now . . ." I couldn't move.

"Now!" he shouted yet again. But it was a futile command; I was undone by the heat of battle.

"What, Jeff, what?" I moaned, petrified by boredom.

"The lava capsule, throw the lava capsule!" he screamed, pulling my car keys out of my pocket and hurling them, grenadelike, into the bushes behind the basketball hoop.

Fortunately, at that moment Jody and Rebecca arrived. Josh spotted his sister over my shoulder and shouted.

"Becky, come quick, Wizgar has stolen Daddy's brain."

"Is Wizgar back from Ibish Mountain?" Rebecca asked, urgently scooting under the slide and sitting down next to Jeff.

"Yes, he's back," said Jeff, who was drawing a map with his finger on the ground. "Look what he did to Daddy." I tried to look OK for my girl. She looked at me and gasped.

"We better be careful or he'll chain us to the wheel of fire," she said.

"Don't worry," countered Jeff, tracing an arrow in the dirt. "If you can get this last crystal from the desert of light, we can warp Wizgar back to the underworld."

Rebecca jumped up, ran in a low Audie Murphy crouch across the playground, dove headfirst into the sandbox, did a Marine crawl across it, leaped out, and rolled over and over to a lamppost. She claimed the crystal, then ran straight back across the lava.

"Six . . . seven . . . eight . . . nine . . ." Jeff counted, reaching out for his mate, "ten," he pronounced as she leapt off the lava to safety on the fence.

I turned and walked away, a sadder and soon-to-be-wiser man. At last Josh, I mean Jeff, had the Chip he deserved. And as I began to forage among the bushes and woodchips, looking for the keys, I saw the metaphorical light.

I was just not a playing Daddy. That was neither good nor bad, just a fact. I also have brown eyes. I remembered my mother saying that even as a child I had a tough time with the idea that the trash cans out back were the castle of The Black Prince. Some fathers can look at their daughters and actually see the queen's crown. Not me. To me, a sweat sock pulled down to the bridge of Rebecca's nose looks like footwear on her head. So I'm not good at fantasy. Maybe I don't think the world requires any polishing. Maybe I think the trash cans are interesting per se.

Suddenly I saw everything in perspective. Some fathers are short. Others are nasty. Some drink too much. Others never say a word. I can't do Animal Lotto. As paternal limitations go, it was no disgrace.

As I rose from the shrubbery, keys in hand, I vowed to accept the destiny of my biology. I practiced my speech. I would just tell the kids that even the Big Guy had his frailties. I was a reading daddy. I was a wrestling, pitching, joke-telling daddy. But, no, I was just not a playing daddy. Wishing just wouldn't make it so. Somehow, I knew the kids would understand.

And you know what? They were better off without me. Who needed an oversized comrade who could never remember which was jail and which was base?

And that's how I got to the Adirondack chair, the cup of coffee, and that copy of the *New York Times*. That's how I got to enjoy the yelp of the kids inventing their world while I got to keep abreast of the standings in the American League East.

LESSONS FROM THE FIRE: OF PATERNITY AND PATTYCAKE

Few parents have the surgical swagger to deal with the problem in such a bold stroke. Even Jody, who is most often willing to be the beautiful princess and sit under the sink until Rebecca, the fairy bird, taps her with her magic wand (ha, some wand, a Number 2 pencil!) has been known to pick up the phone and pretend to be talking to someone at her office rather than play Fireball Island. Indeed, she once went so far as to say, "Becky, Mommy's tired. Ask Daddy to be the dragon." (Let's just say that it was the low point of our history, that I've forgiven her, and that every marriage has its wounds.)

But without the clarity of a position paper on play, you'll be constantly bobbing and weaving. Inevitably, someday you'll have to pick a card, roll those dice, retrieve that crystal. In the immortal words of Joe Louis, you can run but you can't hide.

And so, I offer here, a few survival strategies—some tactical, some psychological—for random games. My hope is that these lessons from the fire can be applied to games similar in spirit to the specific nightmares described herewith.

On War: Nuclear and Worse. Because of a technicality, the editors of the Guinness Book of World Records refuse to endorse it as the longest card game on record, but Josh and I once played "war"—one card each, face up, high man takes pair—for Reagan's entire second term. When the game started, I had to tell my boy that a seven beat a three. By the time it ended he insisted that Reagan was constitutionally vulnerable vis-à-vis Iran-Contra.

In the beginning it was a simple back-and-forth pleasure. But after eight minutes, I loosened my tie. After twelve, I found myself looking at the wide-open windows and wondering why it was so stuffy. There was ebb and flow, to be sure. Sometimes Josh or I would be down to three or four cards. But those few cards were always, God help me, winners—kings, queens, aces—that would get the guy on the ropes back in the endless game. An hour into the game, I imagined myself an old arthritis-ridden pensioner, capable only of flopping a dog-eared playing card from the top of a still-thick stack.

Played straight, "war" is life without parole. Here's the survival tip:

Before the game, put your face cards on the bottom half of your deck where you have access to them when you need them. Then whenever the child plays an ace, pull out a king to *lose close.* Turn your possible winners into losers. In addition to losing close, you've got to *win big.* When he plays a 3 or 4, waste a king to beat it. You choose: Either cheat or prepare for a month-long death march of one-card draw.

Hide and Go Seek by Edgar Allan Poe. Hide and Go Seek is the hideous nadir of "playing." Indeed, until I talked it through with Dr. Littman, I had a recurring Hide and Go Seek dream.

I'm hiding where I always hide—under my desk. Josh is hunting for me, skulking around stealthily, peering into closets, behind curtains and chairs. He walks past me twelve times and never looks in the place where he knows I always hide.

I clear my throat. He goes to check the bedroom.

I fake a sneeze. He peers behind the bookcase in the hall.

I stick my leg out as he walks by. He stumbles over it, gets up, and decides I must be in the kitchen.

I shout out, "Josh, I'm under the desk. If you care for me at all, for God's sake, look under the desk." He scoots into the bathroom. I hear him pulling aside the shower curtain.

Climax: I reach out and grab his leg. The action freezes for an instant. I see the pages/months of a calendar tearing off/flipping by like the thirties-movie time-lapse gimmick. Josh takes off his sneakers, slithers out of both his pants and my grasp, and scoots away, shouting, "Becky, I can't find Daddy. Come help me." Then I'm startled awake by the sudden realization that I'm a hundred and three years old and not under my desk at all but snuggled up in a cherry-wood casket.

"The dream, Hugh?" Jody will ask, knowing the answer, and trying to calm me, putting her hand softly over my heart.

"Yes," I gulp, sucking air like a bilge pump.

"It's all right, babe, it's all right," she'll say, "Olly, olly, oxen-free."

The truth is that now and then even the most ingenious efforts at Hide and Go Seek avoidance will fail and you'll find yourself crawling under the humidifier in the linen closet as "Ready or not, here I come" echoes down the hall. Consider these suggestions for some vaguely productive use of the time in which you're in the fetal position, gasping for air:

- **Observe your hand.** Pretend you're Leonardo. A hand is an astonishing and protean thing. And most often it's too far from our eyes to command attention. But not now. Now, it's four inches from your face. Ponder its architecture close up. Consider the fact that your thumb's position, opposite the rest of your fingers, is the only reason you're an accountant instead of extremely hairy.
- **Chant to yourself, "The kids love this, the kids love this."** With luck a repetitive mantra like this will put you into a hypnagogic trance and you'll forget that you're lying under an appliance.
- **Make a point of noticing the place where one wall meets the other and how the shelf you're under fits snugly six inches overhead.** Appreciate afresh the claustrophobic brilliance of Poe's "The Cask of Amontillado."

When Miss Lucy Had a Baby, Daddy Took a Walk. Pattycake is one area of play that holds particular perils for fathers. Mothers, of course, have the female gene for hand-clapping games. Oh, science hasn't proven it yet, but somewhere on that second x-chromosome there is a Nobel Prize for the picking. There can be no other explanation of their uncanny dexterity with hand jive. Consider that their palm-and-finger fluency makes hash of cultural barriers. You drop a three-year-old girl from Burundi into a preschool in Akron and within six minutes she'll be part of a coven in the corner thwapping away in a billingual variation on "*A, My Name is Alice.*"

Conversely, boys and men are hugely incompetent when it comes to the baroque pattycake patterns and cadences. After watching Josh suffer for a while I told him that pattycake was just one of those things that boys weren't generally good at. Jody, ever alert for any sign of biological determinism, jumped in and told him Daddy was wrong. Some people of both genders were good at it, some were not. It was a question of practice, she continued. If Josh dedicated himself to becoming a master clapper, she concluded, there was nothing holding him back. Nor, she added, was there any reason why Rebecca couldn't grow up to be president of the United States. She was as right about Rebecca as she was wrong about us guys.

Just stay away from this stuff, Dad. We'll never get it. Hell, we invented the simple high-five as a male protest of girlish digital complexity. Don't even bother. There's no upside for anybody. As soon as your eighteen-month-old woman-child stops having trouble hitting your hand, commend her to her mother's estrogenic care.

OF THE NATIONAL PASTIME AND
THE PASSAGE OF TIME

Baseball is, of course, the only game there is. Unlike those miserable, crabbed little dice-rolling desecrations that pretend to recreation, only baseball has the true joyfulness of play. Its statistics make mincemeat of time, linking the flanneled magnificos of Cobb's day with the double-knit deities of ours. It is the most romantic of our games. There is finally something generational about the summer game. "Baseball," wrote poet Donald Hall, "is fathers playing catch with sons."

Before his son reaches five virtually every father in the land will find himself trying to toss a cracked plastic ball so that it hits a red plastic bat. And there's not much overly romantic about a five-year-old taking three futile Ruthian swings and getting good at public failure. So early on, before baseball becomes required, it's up to us to make the memories of sweet summer evenings instead of ball-yard despair. Here are a few tips to help make magic of those moments.

How to Hit a Four-Year-Old's Bat. The central principle is to minimize variables. That begins with the batting stance.

Don't teach the classic. Most fathers—brainwashed to think "slugger"—will show their boys the heroic, old-fashioned flourishes: the statuesque angularity of Teddy Ballgame, the muscular torque of the Mick, the fierce explosion of Reggie, the elbows-high of Yaz. We like to think of the kid as a guy with some thump. Wrong. This child weighs thirty-seven pounds. The point isn't power, it's contact. Stop thinking Canseco; start thinking Charley Lau.

Lau was a banjo hitter for the Orioles and Athletics who turned into a helluva hitting coach. He teaches a flat, minimalist swing that starts with the bat nearly parallel to the ground. The theory is that if you don't have to move the bat down from the vertical plane into the horizontal plane, you minimize the places where something can go wrong. True, Frank Robinson didn't need to minimize anything. But Frank, Jr., does.

So, as you're about to show your son how to stand

and swing for the first time, resist the atavistic inclination toward the dinger. Tell Frank, Jr., to hold the bat nearly straight out, maybe six inches behind the plate. If the bat's out there you've got a chance at hitting it with the ball. Impact, however tame, is what we're after. Believe me, once the boy starts making contact, without a word of advice from you, he'll start inching the bat back to a spot from which he can take a rip. Before you know it your son will have a batting stance all his own. Remember: *You don't teach baseball, you plant it. Let if flower.*

The Poppa Pitch. Also keep in mind: pitch the ball without much arc and with a little pace. The tendency—because the batter is about the size of Dave Winfield's mitt—is to throw a lollipop blooper ball. The problem is that it's much tougher to make an arcing pitch intersect the swing path of the bat. Also, even if there is some contact, there's no distance. Remember the laws of physics. A Clemens fastball disappears in a hurry, a Hough knuckler requires some muscle to get gone.

I'm not recommending that you give junior a taste of the express, but just a nice flat pitch whose speed might turn into something memorable.

How to Buy Equipment. Buy the fattest bat you can find. Biggest ball too. Consider starting with a beach ball. Contact. Contact. Contact.

"And It's One, Two, Three, Four Strikes Yer Out at the Old Ball Game." Perhaps the most important concept of paternal baseball is the "tickie."

A "tickie" is to a foul tip what a quark is to a hydrogen atom. It is the merest intersection of bat and ball, a collision so discrete that only Dad, the steady pitcher, and Scrags, the family spaniel, can possibly hear it.

"Tickies" only happen when a batter who doesn't know all the letters of the alphabet has two strikes. They are called by the pitcher (Daddy) just as a look of despair flits across the peachy face of the batter. They are always disputed by a sullen third baseman who shouts "Strike three!" with an unbecoming glee.

"Tickies" are one more chance, a final swing. Indeed, it is a tribute to the folks who conjured up the game that, while three strikes makes batting a harsh discipline, four tilts the whole game toward offense. When called with affection by Dad, the big right-hander, a "tickie" inevitably precedes a fly ball with possibilities. A "tickie" means life is full of opportunity.

ON BEING A PLAYER

When an athlete refers to a competitor as a *player*, it's a term of understated respect. It means Joe Montana feels the game in his bones, Ryne Sandberg understands its energies, Magic Johnson can be relied upon to go at it straight down the middle. In the roaring '80s, the business world borrowed the phrase to describe an executive up to the challenge.

Since I've been a parent I've aspired to be a player. Not at those dreaded games. No indeed. In fact, I'm more than a little bit proud of my incompetence at ring-o-levio. It proves I have a life and other things clouding my mind. But I would like, at least, to have the *option* of playing in the kids' league. It's clear to me that Josh and Rebecca hear sounds from a wider range of frequencies than I do. Their access to everything—terror, joy, the antic, and the dark—is immediate. Mine is secondhand. No question, the vitality of their spirits outlines the indolence of mine. They get to be druids, I'm Dad.

But if kids are a constant reproach, they are also a round-the-clock goad. They may reveal our worst, but

they also summon our best. Like Dorothy and her com-
panions on the road to Oz, Mom and Dad often discover
brains and heart and courage they never imagined were
in their repertoire. The next generation can raise the
level of your game.

The kids teach what Thoreau called "the gospel according to this minute," the art of life tasted right now
and without translation. Right now. Often, on the playground or by the sink or in any of a dozen daily daddy
venues, I feel the persistent lament of yesterday and the
nagging obligation of tomorrow give way to the present,
the immediacy of the boy assembling himself, on this
nothing-much Tuesday in November. If you're a player,
that moment feels like the forest just before the rain—
extravagant, uncivilized, thrilling, and you had to be
there.

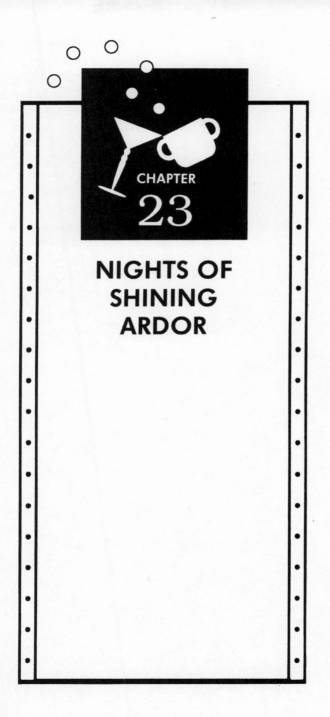

NIGHTS OF SHINING ARDOR

Fourth of July weekend. We had spent three hours on the beach, tending the children at full throttle. Sand castles, sunscreen, Styrofoam surfboards, Popsicles, kites, even a little freedom or speech, every liberty the founding fathers could have imagined. And ahead of us that night loomed a barbecue, fireworks hoisted over the bay, and ice cream in cones, on sticks, in deep dishes, in America. A sweet, salty day was fading to night.

And then, as though on cue, people began folding up beach chairs, searching for sand-sifters, twisting tops onto tubes, shaking out towels and paperback thrillers. In what seemed like an instant we were, the four of us, alone on the beach together.

Great gulls swooped, fluttered down, looking for the rice cake left behind. Josh and Rebecca thwapped along the slick stretch of sand, rousting snails and digging canals. The sun tumbled over the dunes, wrapping, I swear, a halo around Jody, and casting our children in glow.

I plead guilty to a soft spot for the gloaming. In medieval times poets talked of *sweven*, this half-dream state between sleep and wake, the time of clarity. With the kids, somehow the coming of darkness casts us in light. Those last moments of day—the once-more plunge into the surf, the drop in temperature, the rising of the wind—reveal us as an epic no less full of rapture, chivalry, and faith than the *Song of Roland*.

As we packed up in the vast roar of the ocean, to the plaint of the seabirds, my pulse quickened under the

influence of the globe and the children, the unnerving
shiver of beautiful things. I looked up and saw Rebecca
hit Josh with a shell. We were galumphing toward the
car, carrying everything we owned, when Josh dropped
a dime on his sister.

"Daddy, Becky hit me with a shell."

"What kind of shell was it?" I ask, hoping to play
professor instead of judge.

"I don't know, Daddy, but it hurt," he said, not
thrilled with my scientific cast of mind.

"It was a clam shell," Becky said, clearly more proud
of her taxonomy than ashamed of her crime.

"Becky, don't hit your brother with shells."

"Okay, Daddy, I won't hit him with shells."

"Or anything else, Becky, right, Dad?" Josh added,
hip to his sister's ways.

"Right," I said. "Let's go get some ice cream."

Later that night I watched the three of them in the
rockets' red glare, two faces glazed with chocolate and
vanilla, the other tired, tanned, at ease, and on watch,
the face of a mother in America at springtide. I felt like
a gentle barbarian. I felt at that moment as though I
had access to it all, as though I was linked, through the
kids, to all the soft sounds and, on behalf of the kids, to
a ferocious strength. And I felt for an instant like no
more than a vessel for this affection, Not me, wrote
D. H. Lawrence of the poet's voice, not me, but the wind
that blows through me.

I lifted Rebecca into my arms as Independence Day
boomed above us. And in that moment, I felt suddenly
ashamed of my pride and humbled by my good fortune.
This was, after all, no big deal. It was just life. It was
just the commonplace habit of big strong people tending to little weak ones. Nothing more. And in that moment I resolved to a deeper discretion, to ease up on the
children. I vowed to be careful, quiet, less sudden and

quick in sentiment. I vowed to spare them the burden of a father to whom they were breath.

Then, woozy with the day, Rebecca wrapped her arms around me and surrendered into my shoulder. And finally, barely awake, a drowsy, sun-sapped cub, she wiped her ice-creamy hands into the hair on the back of my neck.

God help me, but I heard another call to glory.